Beside the Golden Door

Beside the Golden Door

U.S. Immigration Reform in
a New Era of Globalization

Pia M. Orrenius and Madeline Zavodny

The AEI Press

Publisher for the American Enterprise Institute

WASHINGTON, D.C.

Distributed by arrangement with the Rowman & Littlefield Publishing Group, 4501 Forbes Boulevard, Suite 200, Lanham, Maryland 20706. To order call toll free 1-800-462-6420 or 1-717-794-3800. For all other inquiries please contact AEI Press, 1150 Seventeenth Street, N.W., Washington, D.C. 20036 or call 1-800-862-5801.

NRI NATIONAL
RESEARCH
INITIATIVE

This publication is a project of the National Research Initiative, a program of the American Enterprise Institute that is designed to support, publish, and disseminate research by university-based scholars and other independent researchers who are engaged in the exploration of important public policy issues.

Library of Congress Cataloging-in-Publication Data

Orrenius, Pia M.
  Beside the golden door : U.S. immigration reform in a new era of globalization / Pia M. Orrenius and Madeline Zavodny.
     p. cm.
  Includes bibliographical references and index.
  ISBN-13: 978-0-8447-4332-5 (cloth)
  ISBN-10: 0-8447-4332-1 (cloth)
  ISBN-13: 978-0-8447-4351-6 (pbk.)
  ISBN-10: 0-8447-4351-8 (pbk.)
  [etc.]
  1. United States--Emigration and immigration—Government policy. 2. Globalization—United States. I. Zavodny, Madeline. II. Title.
  JV6483.O77 2010
  325.73—dc22

                                                                    2010019592

14 13 12 11 10   1 2 3 4 5 6 7

Printed in the United States of America

Contents

List of Illustrations

Acknowledgments

First and foremost, we thank Henry Olsen, vice president at the American Enterprise Institute and director of the National Research Initiative, who encouraged us to take on this project and without whom this book would not have been possible. Three anonymous reviewers, along with George Rainbolt and Jason Saving, provided invaluable feedback on a draft of the monograph. We thank them for their time and suggestions. Heartfelt thanks also go to Michael Nicholson, research analyst at the Federal Reserve Bank of Dallas, for research assistance, and to Mark Wynne, director of the Globalization and Monetary Policy Institute, Federal Reserve Bank of Dallas, and Guillermina Jasso, professor at New York University, for helpful discussions. We also thank AEI staff for their help in putting the book together, including Emily Batman and Laura Harbold for their comments and assistance and Anne Himmelfarb for her very careful editing and useful suggestions; any remaining errors are our own.

The authors would like to note that the views expressed here are their own and in no way reflect the views or position of the Federal Reserve Bank of Dallas or the Federal Reserve System.

Introduction

With trade and migration at historic levels around the world, we are in an era of globalization that rivals the start of the twentieth century.[1] During that earlier era of globalization, Emma Lazarus wrote her famous poem "The New Colossus," an engraving of which was mounted inside the pedestal of the Statue of Liberty in 1903. The last line of that poem reads, "I lift my lamp beside the golden door." This invitation to immigrants included a promise of economic opportunity that stretched from New York and the eastern seaboard to the prairies of the heartland and on to the continent's western frontier.

In the late nineteenth and early twentieth centuries, the U.S. economy was growing rapidly, wages were rising, and the need for labor was great. The lure of economic opportunity was not lost on Europeans or Asians, many of whom struggled to survive in their home countries. Once in the United States, Europeans cultivated farmland in the Midwest and Chinese laborers toiled on railroads in the West, while immigrants of all nationalities fueled urban industrialization in the East. Prior to the 1880s, immigration to the United States—and throughout the world—was largely unregulated. The movement of people was limited more by migration costs than by restrictive government policies. The reason seems clear: economic growth was possible only with more workers, and more workers led to higher growth. In the New World, land was abundant but labor was scarce.[2]

Today, economic growth is more rapid in emerging economies than in postindustrial nations like the United States, and populations are again on the move in search of better opportunities. The "New World" of the twenty-first century would likely encompass China and India, not the United States and Western Europe. But workers are moving throughout the world, from "Polish plumbers" and other job seekers on the move from Eastern to Western

Europe to the massive rural-to-urban migrations underway in Asia. If current trends continue, the United States will soon find itself vying with China and India to be the world's economic superpower.[3]

The United States' economic superpower status can be traced back to two periods of growth, 1870–1913 and 1950–2000. Both eras were marked by increased openness that began with rising trade and migration and culminated in greater integration of capital markets. Just as globalization in general and immigration in particular helped pave the way to U.S. superpower status then, they will continue to be key to securing the nation's economic future. Immigrants accounted for almost half of labor force growth in the United States during the last decade, and by 2008 the foreign born comprised nearly 16 percent of the U.S. labor force.[4] These immigrant workers contribute to economic growth in myriad ways. High-skilled immigrants boost innovation and create businesses. Labor supplied by low-skilled immigrants is central to keeping prices low for labor-intensive goods and services that cannot be imported or automated, like construction, child care, and landscaping. Both high- and low-skilled immigrants fill gaps left by the aging native workforce. Indeed, as the U.S. population ages and global competition intensifies, the foreign born will become an even more important source of economic growth.

At the same time as the position of the United States in the world economic order is changing, the composition of Americans is also shifting, shaped in part by immigration policy. Unprecedented numbers of the foreign born— over 21 million people—have come to the United States to stay since 1990.[5] The foreign born comprise about 13 percent of the U.S. population today; the last time the foreign-born share was so high was about one hundred years ago. Whereas new immigrants at the beginning of the twentieth century were primarily from eastern and southern Europe, today's immigrants are predominantly from Latin America and Asia. Hispanics are the fastest growing ethnic group in the United States, and non-Hispanic whites are likely to make up a minority of the population by 2050.[6] Illegal immigration is also at record levels; about one-third of U.S. immigrants lack legal status.[7]

The diversity of the immigrant population creates challenges for the United States. Many immigrants have a low level of education and poor English skills. Almost one-third of foreign-born adults have not completed high school, compared with 12 percent of natives.[8] Over one-half of immigrants report that they cannot speak English very well.[9] Fully integrating these low-skilled and non-English-speaking immigrants into the economy and broader civil society can pose problems. At the same time, however, a higher fraction of foreign-born adults have a post-graduate education than natives, and many of them received this education in the United States. These immigrants have filled gaps in the high-skilled segment of the U.S. workforce, particularly in science, technology, engineering, math, and medicine. Despite the contributions of high-skilled immigrants, for each one who gets to enter and stay in the United States, our current laws turn many more away.

Any serious discussion of immigration must start with documenting its benefits and costs for the United States. Immigration boosts the U.S. economy, spurs innovation, enhances productivity, benefits consumers by keeping prices low, and enriches our society and culture. But current immigrant inflows are disproportionately low-skilled and unauthorized, which leads to adverse effects on the earnings of competing native workers. It also creates an adverse fiscal impact, with low-wage immigrants receiving more in public services than they pay in taxes, on average. Meanwhile, high-skilled and other employment-based immigration is severely limited by quotas and bureaucratic red tape. Immigration policy needs to be reformed to maximize the economic and societal benefits from immigration while minimizing the costs. The United States needs a process that selects the most valued immigrant workers and allocates visas efficiently among them.

The United States is obviously not alone in requiring such a process. Indeed, immigration to the United States is only a fraction of global migrant flows. Each year, between ten and fifteen million migrants leave their homelands for an extended or permanent stay in a foreign country.[10] Almost two hundred million people live outside their country of birth.[11] There are over eleven million refugees, many of whom will never return home.[12] But out of a world population of almost seven billion, migrants are truly the exception and not the rule. This is puzzling. With enormous income gaps between countries, the potential global gains from increased migration are huge, far larger than those from freer trade. The income gains associated with labor migration from low-wage developing countries to high-wage industrialized nations outweigh any potential gains from further liberalization of trade or capital flows by a factor as high as 25 to 1.[13]

Given the magnitude of these potential gains, why does only about 3 percent of the world's population become international migrants? Migration costs are one answer, with some people lacking the funds or information that would enable them to emigrate. But policies and politics play a more important role in limiting migration flows.[14] Uncountable numbers of potential immigrants are stymied by immigration policies that prevent them from entering the country of their choice. Despite the massive global gains that would result from just a modest liberalization of labor migration, policymakers in developed countries focus disproportionately on expanding trade, not migration.[15] The reluctance to liberalize migration stems from the fact that the biggest beneficiaries of migration are the migrants themselves. Natives may benefit on average, as they do from free trade, but the gains are asymmetric, and costs often fall on the most vulnerable groups. Natives also oppose immigration on non-economic grounds, fearing erosion of national identities and common values.

In a world in which millions of people are on the move but policymakers resist opening borders, how should U.S. immigration policy be designed? We argue that the economic future of the United States hinges on bringing the best minds together here. The comparative advantage of the United States lies in technology-intensive, high-skilled jobs that create and disseminate knowledge and spur technological innovation. The most important function of U.S. immigration policy is therefore to admit workers who bring the human capital that will lead to more innovation, faster growth, and higher standards of living. At the same time, however, the United States cannot ignore the important role of low-skilled immigrants who, by diversifying and increasing the size of the workforce, generate gains to specialization and boost natives' living standards. For both high- and low-skilled immigrants, immigration policy should focus on admitting people on the basis of employment, not family ties.

This monograph presents a plan for how to achieve these dual objectives. It proposes abandoning current policy, which has failed along numerous dimensions. Instead of cobbling together piecemeal reforms, this book presents a fresh, comprehensive immigration policy that focuses on admitting the workers most valued by the market in a way that minimizes adverse effects on U.S. workers and funnels migration gains to U.S. taxpayers. The proposed policy is not about raising quotas on the alphabet soup of existing visa programs; rather, it entails a complete overhaul of the current system.

The proposal is designed from an economics perspective and omits a detailed consideration of the social and cultural aspects of immigration. We limit our focus to policy changes regarding employment- and family-based immigrants. Refugee and asylum policy, which is based on humanitarian and geopolitical concerns, not economics, is not discussed here. We also do not touch on the interaction between national security and immigration policy other than to emphasize that immigrants should always be subject to screening and thorough background checks.

In the plan proposed here, employment-based immigration takes precedence over family reunification. Work-based visas are the rule, not the exception. High-skilled foreign workers are initially admitted for five years and can earn permanent residence and then citizenship. Low-skilled workers wait longer but also have a clear pathway to permanent residence and naturalization. Employers need a permit to hire foreign workers; the federal government auctions off these permits. By observing auction prices, the government can gauge demand for foreign workers and adjust the number of new permits in response to changes in labor demand. Fast and accurate employer verification combined with appropriate sanctions is necessary to ensure that illegal immigration is kept to a minimum.

Foreign workers are not tied to a particular employer, reducing the likelihood of employer abuses and keeping compensation at competitive levels. Workers who want to bring over their spouse and children pay a fee to help offset the fiscal cost of such dependents. The plan presented here increases the benefits of immigration to U.S. economic growth and competitiveness while limiting the harms imposed on native workers and taxpayers. Revenues raised from permit auctions and fees allow the federal government to compensate state and local governments and even individual workers for costs imposed by immigration, solving the main political problem that has stymied immigration reform in recent years.

Chapter 1 provides a brief historical synopsis of U.S. immigration policy and an overview of current law, focusing on what is worth keeping and what should be discarded. Chapter 2 discusses the lessons of globalization for immigration reform and outlines the key goals that should underpin immigration policy in the future. Chapter 3 then presents the details of the plan outlined above. Chapter 4 counters potential criticisms of the plan and explains why this plan is superior to a point system or other policies often promoted as potential reforms.

The book's overall goal is to present a selective, flexible, and efficient immigration policy that enables the United States to compete in an increasingly global economy. The new laws have to be comprehensive, covering all immigrants, and reform has to be politically viable, with tangible benefits for voters. We believe that, while not all potential immigrants who knock at the golden door should be admitted, the door should swing wide open to welcome those whose skills and willingness to work hard make the United States a more competitive and prosperous nation.

1

The Challenge: Picking Up the Pieces

U.S. immigration policy is in dire need of reform. Each year, U.S. policies keep out uncountable numbers of the world's best and brightest professionals while allowing hundreds of thousands of low-skilled workers to sneak into the country and work illegally. The vast majority of visas for legal permanent residence are awarded on the basis of family ties, with only a small share allocated on the basis of skills. Add in the strict limits on the number of temporary workers, and the system almost seems designed to limit the benefits of immigration—economic growth and competitiveness—and to amplify its costs.

Under current policy, the fastest track to a permanent resident visa (or "green card") and then U.S. citizenship is to marry a U.S. citizen, not to have the skills the economy values most highly. Today's immigration policy is largely a holdover from the 1960s and is increasingly out of line with our twenty-first-century economy. Since the last major immigration reform in 1965, the U.S. economy has grown by a factor of four and the labor force has more than doubled. Economic activity has been transformed dramatically, shifting from manufacturing to services and becoming more integrated with the rest of the world than ever before. Liberalized trade policies have taken advantage of the openness to new markets brought about by globalization, whereas immigration policies have largely stood in the way.

That said, U.S. immigration policy does do some things right. Postwar immigration laws, passed during the Cold War, sought to win the technology race by bringing the best scientists to the United States via skill-based visas. Although this category of visas was very limited under the 1965 law, it nonetheless proved important to economic growth in subsequent decades, and changes in U.S. immigration law in 1990 increased the number of skill-based visas. But this success has begun to work against the United States, as

Western European countries have copied U.S. skilled worker visa programs and now compete with the United States to attract global talent. U.S. immigration reform therefore becomes increasingly urgent.

Another factor lending urgency to immigration reform is the unceasing inflow of low-skilled migrants. Many are entering the United States illegally, but hundreds of thousands enter legally each year on the basis of family ties. Although the economy benefits from low-skilled foreign workers, these immigrants impose costs as well, particularly on less-educated natives and earlier immigrants who have already been battered by structural change in the economy.

This chapter lays the groundwork for reform by giving an overview of past and present immigration policy and then breaking down the current system into pieces to discard and pieces to salvage. As the federal government crafts immigration reform, it should take careful note of lessons learned to create an immigration policy that is flexible, selective, and efficient, yet humane.

U.S. Immigration Policy: A Checkered Past

U.S. immigration policy has a checkered past.[1] Policy objectives have been a moving target, changing to reflect the economic and political realities of the time. A common early goal was bringing in labor, from indentured servants and slaves in the eighteenth century to settlers and workers more generally in the nineteenth century. But in the late 1800s, when the first laws regulating immigration were passed, the objective of immigration policy switched from attracting workers to keeping certain people out. Family reunification replaced the focus on the workforce only in the mid-twentieth century.

Early laws excluded a variety of undesirable groups. These included criminals and prostitutes (1875), "lunatics" and people likely to become a public charge (1882), and paupers, polygamists, and illiterate adults, among others (1907 and 1917). The Immigration Act of 1907 banned importation of all contract labor except for skilled labor "if labor of like kind unemployed cannot be found in this country," as well as domestic servants and a few professional occupations. Many other early restrictions likewise aimed at protecting U.S. workers from competition by cheaper workers,

---

Box 1-1: An Aside on Terminology

Immigrants in the United States can be divided into four general groups: *naturalized U.S. citizens*, foreign-born people who have passed a citizenship test and met other requirements and have the same legal rights as natives; *permanent residents*, foreign-born people who hold a green card, or visa, that allows them to reside permanently in the United States, but are not naturalized U.S. citizens; *temporary migrants*, people granted entry into the United States temporarily for a specific purpose, including visitors, students, and temporary workers; and *undocumented* (or *illegal*) *immigrants*, which includes people who illegally cross the border into the country ("entry without inspection"), people who overstay a visa, and people who violate the terms of their entry, such as working while on a tourist visa. In official parlance, only permanent resident visa holders are considered "immigrants" while temporary migrants are "nonimmigrants" and undocumented immigrants are "unauthorized immigrants." This book, in contrast, uses "immigrant" in its most general sense to refer to all foreign-born people. It uses the terms "illegal," "unauthorized," and "undocumented" immigrant interchangeably. The discussion of temporary visas here ignores those for visits for business or pleasure and focuses on visas that are conditioned on employment and allow people to temporarily reside in the United States in order to work.

Estimates suggest that, as of 2008, the foreign-born population in the United States totaled 39.9 million people. Of these, 14.2 million (36 percent) were naturalized citizens; 12.3 million (31 percent) were permanent residents; 1.4 million (4 percent) were temporary migrants; and 11.9 million (30 percent) were unauthorized immigrants.[2]

---

particularly those who were nonwhite. Importation of Chinese contract laborers was prohibited in 1875; the ban was expanded to include all Chinese workers under the Chinese Exclusion Act of 1882. The so-called Gentlemen's Agreement with Japan in 1907 effectively ended immigration from

FIGURE 1-1

NUMBER OF LEGAL IMMIGRANTS ADMITTED, 1820 TO 2008

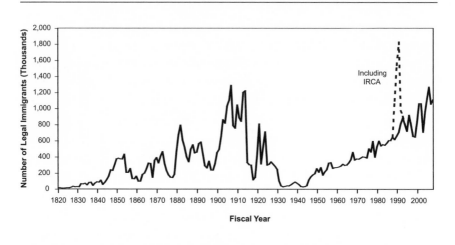

SOURCE: Department of Homeland Security (2009c).
NOTES: These data are an undercount of legal immigrants (permanent residents) and do not include temporary migrants or unauthorized immigrants. In early years, the counts are based on passengers arriving by sea (and thus do not include those entering by land). Land arrivals are enumerated only after 1908 but are an undercount in early years. IRCA = Immigration Reform and Control Act of 1986.

Japan, and the Immigration Act of 1917 barred virtually all immigration from Asia.

At the same time, decreases in transportation costs combined with economic and political upheaval in Europe were leading to dramatic changes in immigrant inflows. As figure 1-1 shows, massive waves of immigrants were arriving in the United States in the early 1900s. More importantly, these inflows were largely composed of southern and eastern Europeans, not the English, Germans, and Irish who had traditionally dominated immigrant inflows.

Laws passed during the 1920s were motivated by xenophobia and high unemployment in the wake of World War I.[3] Faced with a resumption of mass immigration from southern and eastern Europe after the end of the war, lawmakers passed the most restrictive immigration laws in the history of the nation. The 1921 Emergency Quota Act limited annual immigrant inflows to 3 percent of the population, by national origin, present in the United States in 1910. The Immigration Act of 1924 lowered the quotas to 2 percent of the population, again by national origin, present in 1890.[4]

FIGURE 1-2

NUMBER AND SHARE OF FOREIGN-BORN POPULATION, 1850 TO 2008

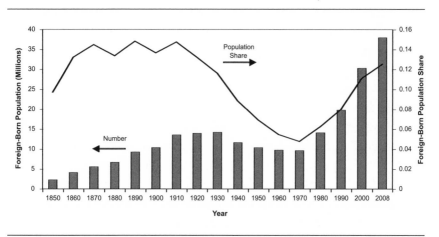

SOURCES: For data from 1850 to 2000: Table 1 of U.S. Bureau of the Census (1999). For 2008 data: U.S. Bureau of the Census, Decennial Programs and American Community Survey.

Lawmakers were essentially attempting to turn back the demographic clock by hugely favoring immigration from western and northern Europe.

Instead, they ushered in a dramatic slowdown in U.S. immigration that would last for over forty years. The mismatch between the nationalities that were allowed to immigrate in large numbers and the countries from which large numbers of people wanted to enter created a stalemate. As a result, the foreign-born fraction of the U.S. population hit a historic low of less than 5 percent in 1970, as shown in figure 1-2. Despite the total population having tripled in size, the number of foreign-born persons was almost as small in 1970 as in 1890, as shown by the bars in figure 1-2.

Policy changes in the immediate postwar period, such as the 1952 Immigration and Nationality Act, left the national-origins quota system largely intact. The changes that were made reflected Cold War priorities: the 1952 law reserved 50 percent of visas within national quotas for "highly skilled immigrants with skills urgently needed in the United States," for example.[5]

A major shift in immigration policy occurred with the 1965 amendments to the Immigration and Nationality Act. These amendments replaced the emphasis on national origin with one on family reunification and created the system essentially still in place today. Employment-based immigration was minimized and regulated because it was thought to create competition for native workers, and family-based immigration—viewed as a moral obligation—was the primary reason to admit foreigners. Hence immediate relatives (spouses, unmarried minor children, and parents) of U.S. citizens were exempt from all quotas. Previously, U.S. citizens' parents had been subject to quotas.

Other immigrants were allocated permanent resident visas based on several admissions preference categories. Two categories were created for employment-based immigrants, four for family-sponsored immigrants, and one for refugees. Each category was allocated a set (but unequal) percentage of numerically restricted visas—not including refugees, about 80 percent were allocated to family members and 20 percent to employment-based immigrants and their dependents.[6] In addition to quotas within each preference class, annual immigration from each country was capped, as were total annual immigrant inflows, not counting immediate relatives of U.S. citizens.

When the 1965 law was enacted, even the proponents of the change considered it a minor event. European immigrants were expected to continue to dominate a relatively small inflow of immigrants. But the law instead marked the beginning of a new era in U.S. immigration because it opened the door to immigrants from countries that truly had surplus labor. This change led to a tremendous surge in the number of immigrants and an unintended shift in their composition.

Chain migration from Asia and Latin America quickly took root, with immigrants from those countries sponsoring relatives who in turn sponsored even more immigrants. The resultant demographic change was dramatic. Figure 1-3 shows the number of legal permanent resident visas issued by region and decade. In the 1950s, Europe accounted for more than one-half of new legal immigrants, Latin America and the Caribbean together made up one-fifth, and Asia made up about 5 percent. By the 1970s, Europe accounted for less than one-fifth of new immigrants, Latin America and the Caribbean for two-fifths, and Asia for one-third. The balance shifted even further in later years as more Latin Americans and Asians became eligible to sponsor relatives and as many Latin Americans in particular legalized their immigrant status under the Immigration Reform and Control Act of 1986 (IRCA).

Viewed in hindsight, this tremendous change in immigrants' region of origin is perhaps not surprising, given the large quotas and quota exemptions

FIGURE 1-3

LEGAL PERMANENT RESIDENT VISAS ISSUED, BY REGION AND DECADE

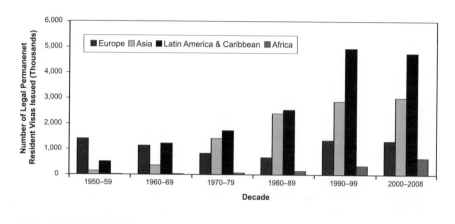

SOURCE: Department of Homeland Security (2009c).
NOTE: The data include IRCA legalizations, creating the spike for Latin America and the Caribbean during the 1990s, but do not include immigration from Canada, Oceania, and "not specified" regions.

granted to relatives of U.S. citizens and permanent residents compared with the relatively small quotas for employment-based immigrants in the 1965 law. It also is not surprising in hindsight that the lack of employment visas for low-skilled workers or a temporary worker program would lead to massive illegal immigration.

Southern hospitality? Mexican immigration to the United States has a unique history. Mexicans (and other southern neighbors from the Caribbean and the rest of Latin America) were notably absent from much of the early period of U.S. immigration history. During 1894 to 1899, official counts show that only 734 Mexicans immigrated to the United States. From 1900 to 1909, this number grew to 31,188, still a low level relative to many other countries at that time.[7]

Northward migration got off to a slow start for two main reasons: the bulk of the Mexican population lived in the center of the country, separated from the border by high mountains and searing deserts; and Mexico had its own labor shortages during the Porfiriato period, which likely made emigration less attractive.[8] On the demand side, it was not until the loss of Japanese labor after the Gentlemen's Agreement in 1907 that U.S. employers began to aggressively court Mexicans, typically by sending contractors deep into Mexico to lure workers northward. In the United States, tight labor markets, the Industrial Revolution, and the expansion of the West created a demand for labor that Mexicans could and did fill.

As a result of labor recruiting and turmoil in the wake of the Mexican Revolution, Mexican immigration grew sixfold between the first and third decades of the 1900s. Despite the fact that many Mexicans returned home once the political situation stabilized, almost half a million Mexicans immigrated legally to the United States during the period 1920–1929. U.S. employers' dependence on Mexican labor intensified when the national origins quotas were passed in the early 1920s and European immigration plummeted. Mexico, along with the rest of the Western Hemisphere, was exempted from those quotas. However, this relatively generous treatment ended abruptly when the U.S. economy collapsed in the 1930s. Mexican immigration ground to a halt, and almost half a million legal Mexican immigrants were deported during the Great Depression.[9]

This story would repeat itself. Once economic growth resumed during World War II and the war effort created labor shortages, the United States government again turned to Mexico for workers. In 1942, the Mexican and U.S. governments crafted the *bracero* program, a temporary worker program which brought in about two hundred thousand Mexican workers per year over the next twenty-two years. The *bracero* program ended in 1964, the year before immigration reform was implemented. Interestingly, as past laws had done, the 1965 law extended special treatment to Mexico. The Western Hemisphere was initially exempted from both preference class and country-specific quotas, and only total annual immigration from the region was capped. Immigration from the Caribbean and Latin America—Mexico in particular—rose steadily.

Changes to immigration laws during the mid-1970s applied the preference category and country quotas universally, and thus included Mexico. Without a large-scale program for seasonal workers, the country cap of twenty thousand visas was clearly insufficient to accommodate the outflow of workers from Mexico—after all, just the number of *braceros* had averaged over 200,000 per year. The late 1970s may well have been the turning point for Mexican immigration to the United States, after which illegal immigration began to dominate northward labor flows.[10] Estimates suggest a net undocumented inflow of about 4.6 million Mexicans in the period 1965 to 1986, during which fewer than 1.3 million Mexicans were granted legal permanent resident status.[11]

The passage of IRCA in 1986 was the result of growth in the illegal immigrant population combined with political whims. The law created two programs under which unauthorized immigrants—estimated to number three to five million at the time[12]—could legalize their status. Almost 2.7 million undocumented aliens, including over two million Mexicans, ultimately received legal permanent resident status under those programs, generating a spike around 1990 (shown with the dashed line in figure 1-1). In order to curb future illegal immigration, IRCA required employers to ask new hires for documents that established their legal status to work in the United States. IRCA also imposed penalties on employers who knowingly hired undocumented workers, increased Border Patrol enforcement and funding, and created a temporary immigration program for seasonal agricultural workers (the H-2A program).

Because it legalized most of the unauthorized population, made it more difficult to enter and work in the United States illegally, and created a temporary agricultural worker program, policymakers believed that IRCA would greatly reduce inflows of undocumented immigrants. As so often happened during the postwar period, lawmakers turned out to be wrong.

Backdrop to current policy. While IRCA focused on illegal immigration, the Immigration Act of 1990 addressed legal immigration and made several changes that increased skill-based immigration. The 1990 law significantly raised the cap on employment-based permanent immigration, from 54,000 to 140,000, and created the H-1B and H-2B temporary worker programs for skilled and unskilled workers, respectively, along with an alphabet soup of other temporary visa categories. However, the law maintained the emphasis on family ties, with immediate relatives of U.S. citizens still not subject to any limits, and relatively large quotas for other relatives. It created two new admissions classes: one for wealthy investors and another for "diversity" immigrants from underrepresented countries. The diversity visa was initially a backdoor to allow immigration by northern Europeans—particularly the

Irish—who did not have close relatives in the United States and could not get skilled visas.

There were two additional important policy changes during the 1990s, the 1996 Illegal Immigration Reform and Immigrant Responsibility Act (IIRIRA) and welfare reform. IIRIRA represented a major policy shift with regard to unauthorized immigrants. In addition to adding more Border Patrol agents and funding a border fence, the law instituted three- and ten-year admissibility bars for immigrants unlawfully present in the United States. As a result, the majority of illegal immigrants who before had been eligible for permanent residence were no longer able to adjust their status.[13] IIRIRA not only called for automatic deportation of noncitizens who had committed crimes but also greatly expanded the list of deportable crimes and applied it retroactively. In addition, the law mandated data collection on foreign students, called for an automated entry-exit system to track foreign visitors, and launched Basic Pilot, an employment verification program that was the precursor to E-Verify (discussed below).[14]

The federal government also enacted welfare reform in 1996. The Personal Responsibility and Work Opportunity Reconciliation Act (PRWORA) restricted the ability of legal immigrants who were not yet citizens to receive means-tested benefits. The law barred most new legal permanent residents from receiving federal benefits for five years or longer (until they naturalize) and allowed states to decide whether to bar legal immigrants from many joint federal and state welfare programs.[15] Although unauthorized immigrants had always been barred from virtually all federal and state welfare programs other than emergency medical care, PRWORA required verification of welfare recipients' legal status.

Recent U.S. legislative attempts. Despite many attempts, the United States has been unable to enact significant immigration reform thus far in the twenty-first century. During the period 2001–2008, some 250 pieces of legislation that included immigration-related provisions were introduced in Congress. Congress tended to pass those laws that increased funding for border enforcement, such as the 2006 Secure Fence Act, not those that sought to overhaul the country's outdated, inefficient immigration policy.

The Comprehensive Immigration Reform Act of 2006 (S. 2611) was perhaps the closest Congress got to passing major immigration reform.

Unlike the parallel House bill (H.R. 4437), S. 2611 included a legalization program for many undocumented immigrant workers.[16] Legalization would require paying a $2,000 fine along with back taxes and application fees, demonstrating knowledge of English and civics, and working for six additional years in order to receive a green card. Undocumented immigrants who had been continuously present in the United States for five years could apply immediately for legalization, while those present in the country for two to five years had three years to depart and apply for readmission, at which time they could apply for legalization. More recent arrivals had to depart immediately and were ineligible for legalization under the bill's provisions.

The bill also required employers to utilize electronic employment verification systems and increased penalties for hiring unauthorized immigrants. S. 2611 created a guest-worker program that would issue annually 200,000 three-year visas that could be renewed once. In addition, the bill included the AgJOBS and DREAM Act legislation, which legalized agricultural workers and certain undocumented minors, respectively.[17] The bill dramatically increased the number of green cards in order to reduce backlogs and accommodate the new applicants.

S. 2611 passed the Senate in May 2006 but was unable to clear the House. The measure failed for two reasons: it could not be reconciled with the harsher House immigration bill, and opponents rallied forcefully against any legislation that was perceived as offering amnesty to illegal immigrants. In opposing the Senate bill, opponents cited the federal government's failure to enforce IRCA's sanctions on employers who hire millions of unauthorized workers.

The following year, a similar bill, the Comprehensive Immigration Reform Act of 2007 (S. 1348), failed to pass in either congressional body. The bill proposed a new "Z visa" to legalize the status of most undocumented immigrants. After eight years, Z visa holders would be able to apply for a green card. The bill created a guest-worker program, with "Y visas" good for two years and renewable after a one-year absence. The bill also eliminated family reunification green cards except for immediate relatives of citizens and instituted a point system to award permanent residence on the basis of age, education, English fluency, occupation, family connections, and possession of a U.S. job offer.

Neither these bills nor other attempts at comprehensive reform passed. In the meantime, enforcement efforts intensified, perhaps with the intention of convincing the public that the government could and would enforce immigration laws. In 2007, the Bush administration implemented a rule giving safe harbor from prosecution to employers who fired workers for whom they had received a no-match letter from the Social Security Administration (SSA). A no-match letter notifies the employer that an employee's Social Security number does not match his name or is invalid, and unresolved no-matches can indicate that the worker is unauthorized. Hundreds of thousands of no-match letters are mailed out every year as a matter of routine, but no action is required of the employer receiving the letter. The Bush rule was enjoined as soon as it came into effect and later rescinded by the Obama administration.

The Bush administration also created E-Verify, a real-time, online verification system that allowed employers to check the legal status of employees against SSA and Department of Homeland Security databases. Participation in the E-Verify system is voluntary for most employers, but required for federal contractors and subcontractors as of September 2009.[18]

The Current Policy Morass

Current immigration policy is complex and inefficient. If nothing else, it has succeeded in spawning a bustling industry of immigration lawyers and consultants. Before we sort through this policy morass to distinguish the good from the bad, we offer a brief overview of the three main categories of people who enter the United States to work and/or reside: legal permanent residents, temporary workers, and illegal immigrants.

Legal permanent residents. The cornerstone of current U.S. immigration policy is the legal permanent resident visa. Permanent resident visas are awarded to five groups of the foreign born:

- Immediate relatives (parents, spouses, and unmarried minor children) of U.S. citizens, who have entered without numerical limit since 1965;

- Other family members, including siblings and adult children of U.S. citizens as well as spouses and children of permanent residents;

- Employment-based immigrants, who are allowed in on the basis of skills or assets or brought in by a U.S. employer;

- Diversity immigrants, who win a lottery open only to persons from certain underrepresented countries, such as many African and European nations; and

- Refugees and asylees, who qualify for permanent residence because they face persecution in their home countries.

All major permanent residence categories except immediate relatives of citizens and refugees and asylees are subject to quotas. Current numerical limits are described in box 1-2.

Green card quotas are important to understand because they result in a highly asymmetric allocation of visas. During fiscal years 2005 to 2008, over three-quarters of new green cards went to family and humanitarian immigrants, and only 16 percent to employment immigrants, as shown in figure 1-4. Diversity and other visas made up the balance. But even this overstates the number of visas going to employment-based immigrants, because the dependents of these immigrants count against the employment-based visa cap. As a result, less than half of employment-based visas (only about 8 percent of all green cards) over the last few years have gone to workers themselves; the rest went to their spouses and children. Spouses are allowed to work if they have green cards, of course, although data on green card recipients at time of admission suggest the majority of these spouses are not in the labor force.[19]

Given the proximity of the United States to developing countries in Latin America and the Caribbean, one major consequence of emphasizing family unification over employment is that many immigrants have relatively low education levels. Data from the 1996 pilot of the New Immigrant Survey—a nationally representative survey of new green card recipients—indicate that mean education levels are considerably lower among immigrants admitted through family ties than employment. Mean years of education was 13.5 among spouses and siblings of U.S. citizens and 7.4 among parents of U.S. citizens versus 16.1 among immigrants admitted under employment-based preferences.[20]

Box 1-2: Green Cards: Current Numerical Limits and Criteria

Immediate relatives (spouses, parents, and unmarried children under age twenty-one) of U.S. citizens are allowed in without numerical limit, while most other green card categories are tightly capped. There is no explicit cap on the number of refugees or asylees who can receive permanent resident status, but the executive branch sets a ceiling on refugee admissions each year.

There are several ways that numerical restrictions are imposed on permanent resident visas. There is an overall annual cap of 675,000 green cards; of these, 480,000 are family based, 140,000 are employment based, and 55,000 are diversity based. Then there are four "preference" classes for family-sponsored immigrants and five for employment-based immigrants, each with its own cap. In addition, immigration from large countries is restricted by country quotas. With certain exceptions, no more than 7 percent (25,620) of family and employment preference visas can go to immigrants from any one country, a cap that is currently binding for natives of China, India, Mexico, and the Philippines.

The preference classes for family-sponsored immigrants (480,000 total) and the minimum number of visas available per fiscal year are as follows:

- First preference (unmarried adult children of U.S. citizens): 23,400

- Second preference (spouses and children of legal permanent residents): 114,200

- Third preference (married children of U.S. citizens): 23,400

- Fourth preference (siblings of U.S. citizens): 65,000

Temporary workers. In much of the post-war period, temporary work visas were granted mainly to seasonal agricultural workers, typically men with little formal education who came from Mexico to work on farms. Currently the United States has two programs for low-skilled seasonal workers:

The preference classes for employment-based immigrants (140,000 total) and the minimum number of visas available per fiscal year are as follows:

- First preference (priority workers, called "EB-1"): 40,040

- Second preference (professionals with advanced degrees and persons with exceptional ability, "EB-2"): 40,040

- Third preference (skilled workers, professionals, and other workers, "EB-3"): 40,040, with at most 10,000 for other workers (those who do not have a college degree)*

- Fourth preference (certain special immigrants, "EB-4"): 9,940

- Fifth preference (employment creation investors, "EB-5"): 9,940

Each class of employment-based visas has its own complex criteria. For example, EB-1 visas do not require a U.S. job offer, while EB-2 and EB-3 visas do. For visas requiring job offers, the employer must comply with a permanent labor certification process (PERM, or Program Electronic Review Management) that requires a thorough search for domestic applicants. The employer must interview all respondents and document why they were not offered employment. Also, foreign workers cannot be paid less than similar native workers and must be paid at least the "prevailing wage." In a typical year, there is a surplus of EB-1, EB-4, and EB-5 visas that are then allocated to EB-3, the category that consistently has the largest number of applicants. The overall demand for employment-based visas has exceeded the cap in every year since 2003.

SOURCE: U.S. Department of Homeland Security (2009a).
NOTE: * The current number of visas for third-preference "other workers" is only 5,000 (and diversity visas only 50,000) because of a provision of the Nicaraguan Adjustment and Central American Relief Act of 1997 (NACARA).

H-2B for nonagricultural workers, which is capped at 66,000 visas per year, and H-2A for agricultural workers, which has no numerical cap but whose onerous requirements and strict work rules limit its use. H-2A and H-2B visas are valid for 364 days and can be renewed twice. H-2B extensions

FIGURE 1-4

SHARES OF LEGAL PERMANENT RESIDENTS BY ADMISSION CLASS
IN FISCAL YEARS 2005 TO 2008

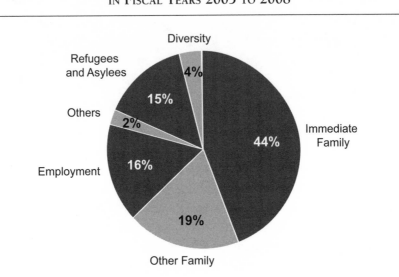

SOURCE: Department of Homeland Security (2009c).

are not counted against the cap.[21] The programs require labor certification by the Department of Labor and impose prevailing wage requirements on employers.

Temporary visas for highly educated workers and professionals, such as the H-1B program, are a much more recent phenomenon but have become wildly popular since their inception. The United Kingdom established a similar program, the Highly Skilled Migrant Programme, in 2002, and in 2009 the European Council adopted the so-called Blue Card directive, which was also modeled on the U.S. experience. H-1B visas bring in skilled workers to work in "specialty occupations," mainly computer programming. H-1B visas for private-sector employers are capped at 65,000 per year, with another 20,000 available for workers who have received an advanced degree from a U.S. educational institution. H-1B visas are valid for three years and can be renewed once. Governmental and nonprofit research organizations and universities are exempt from the cap, as are visa renewals. Employers hiring H-1B workers must attest that they will pay the H-1B worker at least as much as similarly employed U.S. workers.

Visas granted under the North American Free Trade Agreement (NAFTA)—called Trade-NAFTA or TN visas—have requirements similar to those of H-1B visas, but they require nonimmigrant intent and are only for skilled workers from Mexico and Canada.[22] There is no cap on the TN visa program, and the time limit was extended in 2009 from one year to three years. Another popular program for skilled temporary workers is the L-1 visa, which allows multinational companies to transfer workers from overseas to the United States for several years. L-1 visas are numerically unrestricted and are popular in part because they lack the binding cap of the H-1B visas. E and O visas are also temporary visas used to admit skilled workers. E visas go to treaty traders and investors, typically executives in firms that trade with and do business in the United States. O visas are reserved for persons with extraordinary ability in their fields, generally scientists.

Illegal immigrants. In a typical year, at least one-third of new immigrants, or about five hundred thousand persons, bypass immigration laws by violating the terms of a visa or entering the country without inspection. Estimates suggest that the illegal immigrant population in the United States numbers about eleven million.[23] Most of the undocumented came from Mexico, either crossing the border illegally or overstaying a tourist visa. Others came from Central America or Asia, with visa overstays more common than unauthorized border crossings among those from countries far away and arriving by plane.

Jobs are clearly the main driver of illegal immigration to the United States, particularly in the construction sector. Illegal border crossings and apprehensions along the U.S.-Mexico border rise both when the U.S. economy booms and when the Mexican economy crashes.[24] As shown in figure 1-5, apprehensions and U.S. employment growth in residential construction track each other closely. They diverged during the mid-1990s, when the Mexican economy was in turmoil due first to the so-called Tequila Crisis and then to the Asian financial crisis. Inflows of unauthorized immigrants also rise when natural catastrophes occur in nearby countries, such as Hurricane Mitch in Honduras in 1998.

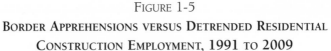

FIGURE 1-5

BORDER APPREHENSIONS VERSUS DETRENDED RESIDENTIAL
CONSTRUCTION EMPLOYMENT, 1991 TO 2009

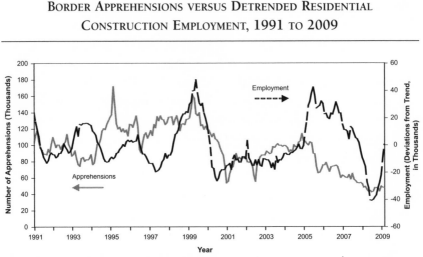

SOURCE: Authors' calculations based on U.S. Bureau of Labor Statistics, Current Employment Staistics Program; U.S. Department of Homeland Security, Enforcement Case Tracking System (ENFORCE) and Performance Analysis System (PAS).
NOTE: Employment is shown as deviations from the long-run trend using a Hodrick-Prescott filter. Employment and apprehensions are seasonally adjusted by the Federal Reserve Bank of Dallas.

Contrary to popular belief, welfare is *not* a magnet drawing illegal immigrants to the United States in appreciable numbers; unauthorized migrants are not eligible for federal or state welfare programs except for emergency medical care. Most illegal immigrants come to work. Indeed, unauthorized immigrant men have the highest labor force participation rate of any immigrant or native group.[25] The majority of these undocumented workers have payroll and income taxes withheld from their paychecks.[26]

What to Keep: The Best Aspects of Current Policy

Although current immigration policy is riddled with problems, the existing system has significant strengths as well. In many respects, it is generous and inclusive. In addition, although policymakers have shied away from comprehensive immigration reform, they have made important small changes to existing programs and processes that have increased skilled migration and temporary work-based visas, have made the system more flexible, and have reduced red tape. Faster processing and portable and renewable visas have led to greater efficiencies and higher productivity as well as enhanced worker protections. Immigration reform should build on these foundations and past improvements that have proven successful.

Inclusiveness. The United States is truly a nation of immigrants. In fact, no other country welcomes so many immigrants.[27] About a million people are granted permanent resident status each year, and another 1.6 million temporary resident visas are issued. Anyone born on U.S. soil is automatically a U.S. citizen, and the naturalization process is relatively straightforward for legal permanent residents who have lived in the United States for several years.

While many Western European countries are far more generous with welfare payments to certain immigrants, in exchange they prohibit or limit immigrant participation in the labor force.[28] The United States is unparalleled in allowing access to its labor market, which helps attract hard-working immigrants. The unemployment rate among immigrants relative to natives is lower in the United States than in any European country.[29] Another upside of working immigrants versus immigrants on the dole, besides the savings to taxpayers, is faster assimilation and less native resentment. In many European countries, the generous welfare and unemployment payments extended to immigrants have fueled resentment and hate acts against foreigners, particularly those from developing countries. Removing barriers to employment also promotes language acquisition and decreases welfare dependency.[30]

The downside of working immigrants versus immigrants on welfare is mainly experienced by competing native workers and the immigrants themselves: life in America is not easy, and many foreigners start out on the bottom, often at a more menial job than they would perform in their home country. Success is correlated with hard work, and if there are bumps on the way, the U.S. safety net for immigrants has many holes in it. Meanwhile, natives who compete with immigrant workers for jobs may also consider open access to the U.S. labor market a downside of U.S. immigration policy.

The United States is also unique in that it confers birthright citizenship on the U.S.-born children of immigrants. This may be an accident of history, given that the Fourteenth Amendment was intended to confer citizenship on former slaves, not immigrants, but it has served the nation well. When immigrants' children are automatically citizens, parents and children alike experience a sense of belonging and have their American identity reinforced. Birthright citizenship has prevented the United States from having second- and third-generation immigrants, something that was common in Germany, for example, until only recently.

Increased emphasis on high-skilled migration. Although the U.S. green card program puts relatively little weight on employment-based immigration, the rise of skilled temporary worker programs has led to a dramatic increase in the influx of high-skilled foreign workers since 1992. Figure 1-6 shows the inflows of high-skilled workers, excluding spouses and children, between fiscal years 1992 and 2008. It shows the number of employment-based legal permanent resident visas and temporary work visas, including H-1B visas and a variety of other categories, issued to high-skilled workers. To avoid double-counting, it includes green cards for new arrivals but not for people adjusting status, since most adjusters initially held temporary work visas.[31] The growth in high-skilled migration is apparent and a result mainly of temporary worker visa programs; the green card plays a surprisingly small role in bringing in high-skilled workers.

H-1B visas experienced particularly rapid growth during the 1990s tech boom as Congress raised the caps to accommodate a dramatic increase in demand by U.S. companies. The H-1B cap rose to 115,000 during 1999–2000 and then to 195,000 during 2001–2003, returning to 65,000 in 2004. Many of these H-1B workers decided to stay in the United States and went on to apply for green cards. The growth in total employment-based green cards since 2000 is mostly a consequence of temporary visa holders adjusting to permanent resident status.[32] There was a surplus of employment-based permanent resident visas after the Immigration Act of 1990 increased the quota for such green cards from 54,000 to 140,000 per year and before the temporary visa programs were fully subscribed. Only after 2003 did the employment-based green card caps become binding. Now they are not only binding; there are also growing backlogs, as discussed below.

Why are temporary worker visa programs so popular? Requirements are less stringent than for employment-based permanent resident visas. For example, labor condition applications (required for H-1Bs) do not require

FIGURE 1-6

VISAS ISSUED TO HIGH-SKILLED WORKERS, FISCAL YEARS 1992 TO 2008

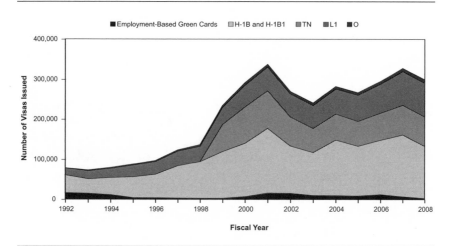

SOURCES: U.S. Immigation and Naturalization Service, Statistical Yearbook (various years); U.S. Department of Homeland Security, Yearbook of Immigration Statistics (various years); Department of State, Report of the Visa Office (various years).

interviewing domestic applicants, whereas labor certification (required for many employment-based green cards) does. Processing is also much faster. Until recently, the Department of Labor needed several years to complete labor certification. Only then could the green card application proceed over to the Department of Homeland Security for the next stages of the approval process. For temporary worker visas, labor condition applications typically take just days to be approved and DHS processing only one to two months.[33] And, unlike employment-based green cards, all H-1B visas are allocated to workers; accompanying spouses and children are in a separate category that does not count toward the cap.

More temporary visas for seasonal workers. The number of work-related temporary and permanent visas available to low-skilled workers is also higher than two decades ago. Of course, most low-skilled workers arriving legally or adjusting status are admitted because they are relatives of U.S. citizens or permanent residents, not because of their work credentials. Nonetheless, as figure 1-7 shows, the total number of work-related visas

FIGURE 1-7

VISAS ISSUED TO LOW-SKILLED WORKERS, FISCAL YEARS 1992 TO 2008

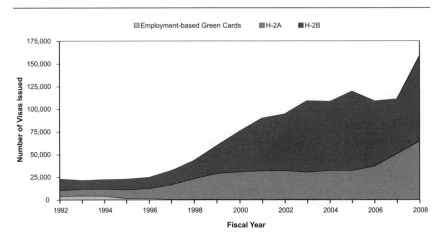

SOURCES: U.S. Immigration and Naturalization Service, Statistical Yearbook (various years); U.S. Department of Homeland Security, Yearbook of Immigration Statistics (various years); Department of State, Report of the Visa Office (various years).

issued to low-skilled workers has risen almost sevenfold since 1992, all due to growth in the number of temporary visas (H-2A visas for agricultural workers and H-2B visas for other seasonal workers). Providing temporary worker visas to low-skilled workers from neighboring countries, such as Mexico, reduces the incentive to migrate illegally. It also preserves circularity, or return migration, the benefits of which are discussed in chapter 2.

Other improvements in permanent and temporary worker programs. In recent years, policy changes have reduced certain backlogs, increased visa portability and renewability, and extended H-1B visas for workers with pending green card applications.

Backlogs have long plagued the employment-based green card program, particularly for categories that require labor certification from the Department of Labor before the application can proceed to the Department of Homeland Security. The 2005 move to PERM, a program of labor certification that eliminated supervised recruitment of domestic workers, marked a significant improvement in the process. PERM allowed employers to attest that they had recruited native workers and to submit paperwork electronically, which reduced the time for labor certification from between three and five years to between six and eight months.

Important changes have also been made to the H-1B and H-2 temporary worker visa programs.[34] H-1B and H-2A visas are now portable across employers, although the new employer must file paperwork with the federal government. Even workers with an approved employment-based permanent resident visa application can now switch employers, assuming they can find a new employer sponsor.[35] Portability reduces the likelihood of employer abuse and increases workers' bargaining power. Previously, H-1B holders were essentially indentured servants tied to a particular employer for six years. By allowing visa holders to move to better job opportunities, portability can help reallocate workers to sectors or areas with unmet demand for labor. This reallocation reduces bottlenecks, allows markets to function better, and provides for better matches between employers and workers. Extending portability to H-2B visa holders is an important, albeit relatively minor, change that policymakers could easily enact.

Another important improvement in temporary worker programs is that H-1B and H-2 visas are now renewable. Since legislation enacted in 2000, H-1B holders have been able to renew their visa for a second three-year period. H-2A and H-2B visas are renewable for two additional one-year periods. Renewability is important since it encourages both firms and workers to make specific investments that increase productivity but might not be cost-effective in the very short run. Employers also have greater flexibility to petition for multiple unnamed H-2A or H-2B workers when the beneficiaries are outside the United States, which is another step toward a more rational policy.

Finally, H-1B visa holders who are prevented from adjusting to permanent resident status under employment-based preferences because of the country cap are now allowed to extend their H-1B status until a visa number becomes available. This is important, given how long the queues are for countries that supply large numbers of high-skilled immigrants. As of March 2010, the queue for third-preference employment-based visas (skilled workers, professionals, and other workers) from India stretched back to applications filed in July 2001; for China, to December 2002. Queues for second-preference employment-based visas are shorter: back to

February 2005 for India and July 2005 for China.[36] As discussed in the next section, these lengthy queues result from country and category caps on the number of visas available each year. Eliminating these quotas and queues is one of several crucial areas for reform.

What to Reform: The Worst Aspects of Current Policy

The three biggest failures of current U.S. immigration law are the disproportionate focus on family-based migration at the expense of skill-based migration; the rigid quota system and the lengthy queues that ensue from it; and the policies that have encouraged massive illegal immigration.

The economic and human costs of current immigration policies are large and, most vexingly, avoidable. Immigration policy could be used strategically to advance national interests and, in that regard, current policy represents a wasted opportunity. Family-based migration, which reunites U.S. citizens and permanent residents with loved ones born or living elsewhere, is the highest priority under current law, even though that focus serves the interests of only a small minority of natives and prior immigrants. Family-based migration induces chain migration, meaning that these flows are self-perpetuating and grow exponentially with each iteration. Reuniting families is an important function of immigration laws, but should not come at the expense of other forms of immigration with more far-reaching benefits.

The nation's interests are equally ill served by the outrageously complex and nonsensical system of quotas and queues the government employs to ration permanent and temporary visas. Rigid, outdated quotas impose baseless caps on visas and, as the demand to immigrate grows, so do the queues. Under the quota system, more of one type of immigration means less of another. What little employment-based immigration there is has been limited mainly to highly skilled workers, those with a bachelor's degree or more. Essential workers who lack formal education credentials but have good job prospects resort to immigrating illegally as a result. Policymakers have to date largely accommodated these illegal inflows by not providing any legal alternatives and not enforcing laws already on the books.

Not enough skill-based immigration. Under current law, skill-based immigration is severely limited despite overwhelming evidence of its many benefits. Moreover, many immigrants who are admitted because of their skills are mismanaged under a temporary visa program that is increasingly incompatible with the caps on the permanent resident visa program.

U.S. immigration laws allocate the majority of permanent resident visas to family-based migration—almost two-thirds in a typical year.[37] Meanwhile, workers who apply for employment-based green cards have to scramble for well less than a hundred thousand green cards. Because the overwhelming majority of employment-based immigrants have at least a bachelor's degree as well as an enthusiastic U.S. employer sponsor, they have relatively high incomes, work in industries and regions where native labor is relatively scarce, and pay more in taxes than they use in public services. In other words, they are a boon to the U.S. economy.

Skill-based immigration is a win-win for the host country and the immigrant.[38] As we indicated in the introduction, educated immigrants tend to work in knowledge industries where their participation in research and development keeps the United States on the innovation frontier. Their discoveries and research activities may have positive spillovers on natives, making natives more innovative as well. The resultant productivity gains pay off for everyone in the long run, raising U.S. living standards and enhancing U.S. competitiveness. In the new era of globalization, when physical capital can be invested anywhere, the key to long-run sustainable growth is recruiting and retaining *human* capital.

The United States is currently in the enviable position of facing a surplus of potential high-skilled immigrants. Yet our country eschews these talented workers and allocates a highly disproportionate share of permanent resident visas to individuals with family ties. These individuals face no education or language requirements and, among the less educated, represent a net fiscal burden to U.S. taxpayers. In fact, about 47 percent of households headed by an immigrant with at most a high school diploma receive at least one means-tested welfare benefit, versus 30 percent of households headed by a native with at most a high school diploma.[39]

Some of the asymmetry in current immigration law has been addressed with temporary worker programs, such as the H-1B visa program. However, the incompatibility of the H-1B program design with the green card program has given rise to new problems. The H-1B program has brought in millions of high-skilled foreign workers whose visas now allow for "dual intent," so that they can begin the lengthy green card process while working under an H-1B visa. But many H-1B visa holders are still waiting for green cards when the six-year visa period ends. Far more H-1Bs are admitted each year than can be accommodated under the employment-based green card program. In fact, estimates suggest that the employment-based green card queue had some 1.2 million people waiting in it as of September 2006, a number that has probably only increased since then.[40] Given the current cap of 140,000 employment visas per year combined with country quotas, the queue extends over a decade. While changes in the program now allow H-1B workers to remain here and work while their permanent resident visa paperwork is in the queue, the uncertainty and lags may deter an uncountable number of potential high-skilled migrants.

An additional inefficiency of the H-1B program is that spouses of H-1B workers are not allowed to work at all. These spouses, who are admitted on an H-4 visa, are barred from the labor force unless they themselves receive a temporary work visa or until they get a permanent resident visa. This rule leaves tens of thousands of potential workers, mostly female and highly educated, sidelined for years, and it makes the United States a less attractive destination for two-career couples. Spouses of other temporary workers (such as intracompany transferees, exchange visitors, and diplomats) are allowed to work, so this rule makes little sense.[41]

Employment-based immigration is also problematic when it comes to admitting low-skilled immigrants. The United States admits large numbers of low-skilled immigrants via family-sponsored preference categories, but these immigrants are not necessarily the workers desired by employers. In addition to having relatively low education levels, immigrants admitted on the basis of family ties are predominantly female, disproportionately elderly, and more likely to be unemployed than those admitted under employment-based preferences.[42] There is little room for employers to bring in low-skilled workers on either a temporary or a permanent basis. This results in huge inflows of undocumented immigrants, as discussed below.

Quotas and queues. Quotas have been policymakers' preferred immigration policy tool since the 1920s. The United States has quotas for the total number of immigrants and then for almost every kind of immigrant, whether workers, siblings, parents, spouses, permanent, or temporary. There are also country quotas, diversity quotas, and private-sector quotas. With the exception of refugee admissions quotas, immigration quotas are rarely changed and have had a predictable result: extensive queues.

We have already discussed the problems that result from limiting employment-based permanent resident visas. But the problems with quotas and associated queues go far beyond the inefficiencies listed above. One particularly nonsensical quota is equal caps on the number of permanent resident visas issued annually by country. Every country, from tiny Djibouti to populous China, is limited to 7 percent of the total number of family and employment preference visas, or 25,620 a year. Although in some sense this rigid equality may seem fair, it leads to wait times of more than a decade for some potential immigrants from China, India, Mexico, and the Philippines, while not affecting those from, say, Lithuania or Luxembourg. Almost one million family-sponsored immigrants from Mexico were in the green card queue as of January 2009, a number that will take at least a generation to clear.[43] If the purpose of the country caps is simply to prevent particular countries from dominating the inflow, that goal is largely undone anyway by unlimited immigration of immediate relatives of U.S. citizens. The country caps fail to take account of distance, economic development, population size, and the number of family ties to people already in the United States.

More generally, the rigid nature of the quota system is problematic. The number of preference-based visas is essentially fixed, changeable only by an act of Congress. The only flexibility in family-sponsored and employment-based permanent resident visa caps consists of adjusting the number of visas in a given year to offset large or small numbers of immigrants admitted the previous year.[44] Similarly, the number of H-1B and H-2B visas (plus some other, very narrow categories of temporary worker visas) is set by Congress and is not generally responsive to changes in either labor supply or employer demand.

The current system makes no attempt to alter the number of visas in response to market forces. Quotas do not increase when the United States economy is booming and better able to absorb immigrants, and correspondingly do not decrease when the economy is contracting. Quotas also do not change in response to changes that would affect people's desire to emigrate, such as economic or political crises in major sending countries. Because of the lengthy queues, immigrants can end up entering in different economic conditions from those anticipated when they began their paperwork. Yet given the length of the queues and the associated uncertainty, it rarely would make sense for a potential immigrant to refuse a visa when his number finally came up, no matter how weak the U.S. economy. The result is that the number of new permanent immigrants is largely unresponsive to the business cycle.

The number of temporary visas is in theory more responsive to the business cycle. However, this responsiveness is limited by the binding nature of the current caps, particularly during economic expansions. Nearly 163,000 petitions were received during the initial week of the 2009 filing period for the 85,000 H-1B skilled worker visas available, for example.[45] It required the combination of a very high cap (195,000) in 2001–3 and the dot-com bust to make the number of H-1B visas issued actually responsive to the business cycle and for H-1B visas to remain available all year. Similarly, the quota for H-2B visas for the second half of fiscal year 2009 was reached in January 2009 despite the economic downturn. When the caps are set at extremely low levels—as they are currently—they can be binding regardless of whether the labor market is tight or slack. Tying the caps to some measure of economic activity would make immigrant admissions more responsive to the business cycle.

Two final quota-related oddities merit mention. First, the H-1B program has a quota for the private, but not the public, sector. This effectively caps labor supply in the sector that is more exposed to market forces, while leaving it unlimited in the sector that is more insulated and is subsidized by taxpayers. And with the trend toward more basic research in the private sector, such discrimination against private-sector employers seems likely to slow innovation. Second, the diversity visa program, which offers permanent resident visas to people from "underrepresented" countries (mainly Europe and Africa) on the basis of a lottery, is an example of immigration policy at its most absurd. From an economic perspective, it makes no sense to randomly award green cards.[46] Why pick a random immigrant when you can choose the best immigrant? It is unclear that the diversity gained under this system serves the national interest or even makes any difference at all. If policy is going to award green cards to immigrants who will make the nation more diverse rather than to those who have been queuing for a decade, then there should be some evidence that immigrant diversity truly does serve the national interest.[47]

Policies toward undocumented immigration. Despite all the problems with hiring high-skilled foreign workers, U.S. employers who demand them at least have several options under the law. In contrast, employers seeking low-skilled foreign workers have very few legal options. Existing temporary worker programs are for seasonal workers only, and the number of permanent resident visas for low-skilled "other" workers is minuscule (currently 5,000 per year). This leaves employers in the service, construction, and manufacturing sectors largely unable to recruit legal foreign workers. Over the years, the combination of strong demand for low-skilled foreign workers, a shortage of visas, and lax enforcement of existing laws has led to large flows of unauthorized immigrants. Demand for low-skilled foreign workers has stemmed in part from the fall in the supply of low-skilled native workers. The number of U.S. workers with less than a high school degree fell by 2.3 million between 1996 and 2008, a decline of 26 percent. The number of native-born workers with only a high school degree fell by 1.3 million, a 4 percent decline.[48]

The federal government began to seriously address illegal immigration in 1993, using aggressive border enforcement such as Operation Hold-the-Line in El Paso and, in 1994, Operation Gatekeeper in San Diego. While the Border Patrol was successful in stopping illegal border crossings where it chose to implement its new strategy, illegal immigrants simply circumvented enforcement by crossing elsewhere along the border. Yet the Border Patrol has been successful in raising the costs of border crossings. Not only have the dollar costs of smuggling risen fourfold since the early 1990s, but more migrants are also paying with their lives: research documents a clear link between increased enforcement and deaths among people trying to cross the U.S.-Mexico border.[49]

Border enforcement is an extremely costly and inefficient way to address illegal immigration. The federal government spends billions of dollars each year to secure the border. Indeed, under President George W. Bush, funding for the Border Patrol increased by 146 percent and the number of enforcement personnel approximately doubled.[50] Despite the build-up along the

FIGURE 1-8

BORDER APPREHENSIONS AND AGENTS ALONG U.S.-MEXICO BORDER, 1975 TO 2009

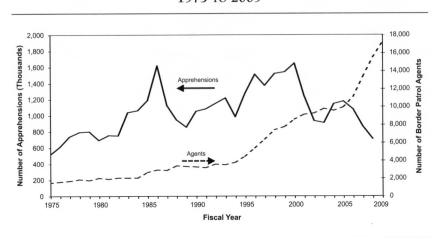

SOURCES: Apprehensions data from the Department of Homeland Security, Enforcement Case Tracking System (ENFORCE) and the Performance Analysis System (PAS). Agents data from http://trac.syr.edu/immigration/reports/143/include/rep143table2.html and are for September of each year. Post-2004 agent data from the Department of Homeland Security, Customs, and Border Protection, Office of Border Patrol.

U.S.-Mexico border, however, apprehensions actually fell in all but two years during the period 2000–2007 (see figure 1-8). Of course, supporters of current Border Patrol efforts can argue that fewer apprehensions are a sign that border enforcement is actually working and deterring potential unauthorized immigrants. Deterrence is doubtless at work, but research suggests economic factors—the rewards of getting into the country—trump enforcement efforts. Increased border enforcement has a bigger effect on where and how unauthorized immigrants cross the border, on the cost of coyotes (smugglers who help people cross the border in exchange for a fee), and on the number of attempts it takes before making it across, than it does on the actual inflow of illegal immigrants.[51]

It is also the case that while border enforcement may keep some migrants out, it raises the reward to those who get in. Paradoxically, it can lead to larger numbers of undocumented migrants inside the United States. Research suggests that undocumented immigrants from Mexico lengthen their duration of stay in the United States when border enforcement increases. This occurs because stricter border control makes it more difficult to cross the border, encouraging some migrants who would leave and later return to just stay instead. It also makes it more expensive to cross the border, causing migrants to stay longer in order to recoup higher coyote fees.[52]

The key to curbing illegal immigration is interior enforcement. Partly as a result of 9/11, the federal government began to get serious about cracking down on unauthorized immigrants and their employers during the 2000s. Interior enforcement has risen dramatically, with well-publicized raids involving major employers such as Wal-Mart and Swift and increased attempts to verify documents. Work-site arrests of undocumented workers tripled between 2005 and 2006 and rose again in 2007. Interestingly, one of the most effective measures against undocumented workers in recent years may have been the Social Security Administration's no-match letter program discussed earlier in this chapter. Although not explicitly created as an enforcement program against illegal aliens, it led to hundreds of thousands of undocumented workers being fired or quitting and, combined with other interior enforcement measures, appears to have reduced the relative earnings of undocumented immigrants.[53] E-Verify, also discussed above, has the potential to be another effective means of interior enforcement. Such policies may reduce illegal immigration by removing the jobs magnet. Of course, there will always be sectors that even interior enforcement cannot reach, such as private household employment. In these cases, border enforcement does play an important role.

Conclusion

The United States has long been in the enviable position among nations of being able to choose its immigrants. Despite this golden opportunity, immigration laws have not kept up with the nation's changing priorities. As long as the United States faces a surplus of foreigners who want to enter, many among the best and brightest in the world, immigration policy should be crafted so as to bring and keep them here. The preference system designed forty-five years ago as part of the 1965 immigration reform is outmoded in this era of globalization and heightened competitiveness.

While the nation and the economy have evolved, immigration law has been largely stagnant, leading to massive illegal immigration, restricted high-skilled migration, and a highly inefficient quota system and lengthy queues. The disconnect between foreign worker inflows and immigration quotas has at times created crises and led to short-sighted and chaotic law-making; witness IRCA and IIRIRA. More recently, lawmakers have addressed immigration problems with stopgap and piecemeal measures rather than forging a comprehensive immigration system that is flexible enough to respond to economic and demographic changes as they occur; selective enough to create slots for the best and brightest, and transparent enough to natives and immigrants to inspire confidence and generate public support. Creating such a system requires that we clearly understand the goals of immigration reform and how to achieve them. It also requires convincing natives they should support comprehensive immigration reform. The way to achieve an efficient, effective immigration policy is discussed in the next two chapters.

2

The Goal: Pro-Growth Immigration Policy

Current immigration policies should be abandoned and a completely new system put in place that emphasizes the types of immigration likely to yield the broadest benefits for the nation today and in the future. The United States should create a viable and coherent immigration policy that prioritizes long-run economic growth by competing globally for talent. The system we describe later in this book is such a policy. It focuses on bringing in immigrants who are in demand; establishes a system of laws that are flexible, yet enforceable; creates an allocation system that limits harm to U.S. workers and taxpayers; and curbs illegal immigration.

Immigration reform along these lines incorporates the new realities the United States faces and avoids repeating mistakes of the past. The forces of globalization are inescapable; as in the late nineteenth century, international mobility of labor and capital is increasing steeply as transportation and communication costs are falling but income differentials persist. Labor markets are no longer constrained by national boundaries, particularly for high-skilled workers, and for good reason. Global labor markets help industrialized nations tackle some of the most difficult challenges they face in the twenty-first century: spurring innovation and maintaining productivity growth; slowing the pace of demographic change; and addressing labor shortages in certain occupations, industries, and regions.

If designed and implemented correctly, a new immigration policy will help secure the nation's future prosperity. Unfortunately, the public debate about immigration policy focuses almost exclusively on mistakes of the past, namely undocumented immigration and the failure of IRCA to put a stop to it. The consensus appears to be that there are few problems with current policy regarding legal and temporary migration, and that the only reform needed vis-à-vis legal immigration is changing the number of available visas.

**Box 2-1: Should Migration's Benefits and Costs
Be Measured Nationally or Globally?**

What constitutes optimal migration policy depends entirely on the perspective of the policymaker. This book takes a U.S.-centric view and evaluates U.S. immigration policy on the basis of economic gains to the United States. We adopt this approach since passing immigration reform will ultimately require the support of the American public.[1] Whether this is the proper stance from a moral perspective is beyond the scope of this book.[2]

Our approach has several implications. First, we generally do not consider the benefits of immigration that accrue to the migrant. Second, most of the discussion ignores effects on sending countries (or other immigrant-receiving countries). For example, we recommend increased levels of high-skilled immigration and ignore the potential harm of "brain drain" to sending countries.

When formulating policy, home and host countries tend to exclude from calculations the gains to the welfare of the migrants themselves. Yet migrants are actually the largest beneficiaries of voluntary migration. Why then ignore their gains? The home country excludes migrants' welfare gains because they are no longer residing there. The host country excludes migrants' welfare gains because the act of migration has already taken place. Only a global policymaker in charge of maximizing the welfare of everyone irrespective of national boundaries would include the welfare gains to migrants themselves in formulating a migration policy. What would such a policy look like? A simple neoclassical model suggests it would enable resources to move to where they are scarce and

---

Immigration reforms considered by the House of Representatives and the Senate in the post-9/11 era have focused on pathways to legalization, border security, and interior enforcement.

But even if illegal immigration could magically be halted tomorrow, most of the problems that arise from current immigration policy would persist. Ending illegal immigration would not boost the number of high-skilled workers who migrate to the United States, and hundreds of thousands of

command a relatively high price. Labor would flow to capital-rich countries and capital would flow to labor-rich countries. Immigration in this case is typically a win-win for both home and host countries as well as for the migrants themselves. U.S. recruitment of workers from Mexico during World War II is an example of this type of immigration; South and Southeast Asians who work on temporary contracts in the Middle East and send back remittances that foster economic development at home offers a contemporary example.

In a model that distinguishes between high- and low-skilled labor, high-skilled labor should flow to where its returns are the greatest. This should be to developing countries, where high-skilled labor is scarce. But in actuality the flow is more often the reverse, with high-skilled labor moving from developing to developed countries. The reasons are many, including home-country problems (such as the poor quality of institutions, corruption, and safety concerns) and host country policies (such as generous research and development funding and liberal immigration laws). In these circumstances, immigration benefits the receiving country and the migrant but may harm the sending country. The case of brain drain, in which high-skilled workers emigrate from developing countries, is a familiar one.[3] While brain drain has typically been understood to harm the home country, recent research has brought its benefits to light. Global labor markets raise skill prices in developing countries, which encourages students to invest in more education.[4] High-skilled migrants facilitate technology transfer to the home country, send remittances, and may return-migrate as well, starting businesses and investing capital acquired abroad.[5]

low-skilled immigrants would continue to enter under the family reunification provisions of current law. Changing who comes to the United States and how immigration affects the economy requires more than reducing the number of undocumented immigrants. True comprehensive reform needs to encompass legal as well as illegal immigration, and not just the number of immigrants but also how immigrants are selected, visas allocated, and laws enforced.

This chapter describes the appropriate goals of immigration in an era of globalization and in light of the economic and fiscal impacts of immigration. The objectives form part of an immigration policy that is pro-growth, politically palatable, and attuned to the changing position of the United States in an increasingly globalized world. The goals laid out here motivate the specific reforms proposed in chapter 3. First, box 2-1 discusses the building blocks of crafting immigration policy, namely how to measure immigration's benefits and costs.

A New Era of Globalization

Globalization shrinks the world by bringing nations closer together through trade, shared financial markets, and migration. Income growth, technological innovation, and government policies all speed globalization's pace.[6] Income growth increases demand for imports. Technological progress reduces effective distances by lowering the costs of transporting people and goods, of communicating and obtaining information, and of outsourcing services. In the nineteenth century, the railroad, steamship, and telegraph had dramatic effects because each lowered the costs of transportation and communication. In the twentieth century, the jet engine, Internet, and myriad other inventions similarly transformed personal and business life. Whether one considers the cost of an international phone call or freight shipping, the magnitude of the declines over time is stunning.[7]

Government policies also play a role in globalization. The repeal of the Corn Laws in Britain in 1846 and the use of the most-favored-nation clause in the Cobden-Chevalier Treaty of 1860 ushered in an era of growing international trade. The expansion of trade agreements and relaxation of capital controls have similarly accompanied globalization one hundred years later. The General Agreement on Tariffs and Trade (GATT) and later the World Trade Organization (WTO), NAFTA, and the European Union (EU) were instituted in the postwar period and sped globalization along. The opening up of China in 1979 and the end of the Cold War in 1989 also marked historic shifts toward more international openness and exchange.

FIGURE 2-1

MEASURES OF GLOBAL ECONOMIC INTEGRATION, 1970 TO 2006

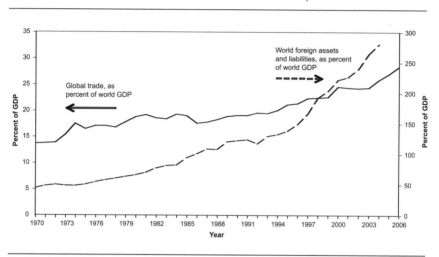

SOURCES: Global trade data (based on exports) and world GDP from World Bank (2009). World foreign assets and liabilities data from Lane and Milesi-Ferretti (2006).

As a result of increases in wealth, as well as technological and policy changes, economies are much more integrated and interdependent today than they were just a few decades ago. This integration has encompassed trade in goods and services and international flows of capital. Global trade in goods and services as a percentage of total output doubled between 1970 and 2006, rising from 14 percent to 28 percent of global gross domestic product (GDP) (figure 2-1). International capital flows grew much more rapidly, however, and estimates of holdings of foreign assets and liabilities jumped from 44 percent of world GDP in 1970 to 280 percent in 2004.[8] Foreign assets and liabilities include portfolio equity investment (company shares), foreign direct investment (FDI), external debt, and official reserves. As can be seen in figure 2-1, financial globalization increased markedly in the late 1990s and 2000s. The bulk of the increase is accounted for by industrialized countries, not emerging markets.

Global trends are reflected in the U.S. experience. Exports and imports increased from 11 percent of U.S. GDP in 1970 to 30 percent in 2008, while U.S. foreign assets and liabilities grew from less than 30 percent of

FIGURE 2-2

MEASURES OF U.S. ECONOMIC INTEGRATION, 1970 TO 2008

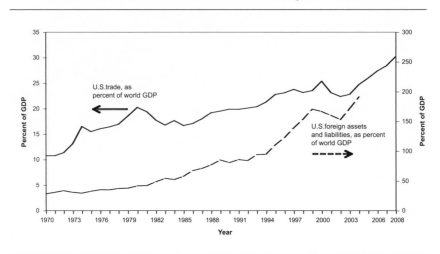

SOURCES: Trade data from the Bureau of the Census, Foreign Trade Data Dissemination; GDP data from the Bureau of Economic Analysis, National Economic Accounts; U.S. foreign assets and liabilities data from Lane and Milesi-Ferretti (2006).

U.S. GDP in 1970 to almost 200 percent in 2004 (figure 2-2).[9] The United States incurs a substantial trade deficit—with imports exceeding exports by some $696 billion in 2008 and $381 billion in 2009—and a corresponding surplus in its financial account, with foreign purchases of U.S. assets far outstripping U.S. purchases of foreign assets. Although this imbalance has troubling aspects, it also suggests that the world finds the United States an attractive place to invest. This may be changing as countries that hold the bulk of U.S. government debt, such as China, express increased concern over U.S. fiscal and monetary policies during the 2008–2009 financial crisis and their implications for the future value of the dollar.[10]

The benefits of globalization occur on many levels. Increased trade results in greater specialization across nations, which leads to improved allocation of resources, lower costs, and higher output. Greater efficiencies generally lead to lower prices—whether of goods, services, or financial products. More competition and greater economies of scale provide similar benefits, while closer integration can also speed knowledge spillovers and technology transfer from industrial to developing countries.

FIGURE 2-3
GLOBAL MIGRATION AND REMITTANCE FLOWS, 1970 TO 2008

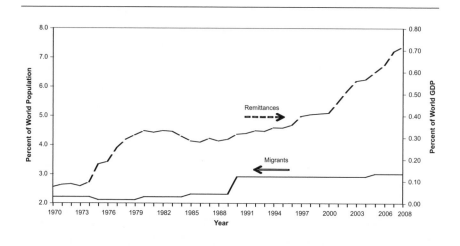

SOURCES: Migration data through 2005 from United Nations (2006) and post-2005 data from United Nations (2008). Remittance data from World Bank (2009).

Nations have, for the most part, agreed that the long-run benefits from free trade and capital flows outweigh the short-run adjustment costs of opening up their economies. As a result, developing nations such as Mexico and China have dumped their restrictive trade regimes in favor of freer trade. This trend is facilitated by multilateral trade agreements and global institutions like the GATT and the WTO that allow member countries to trade with each other at reduced tariffs. Today, 153 countries are members of the WTO, and those that are not, such as Russia, are vying to join. There are clear benefits of expanded international movement of goods, services, and capital.

There are also clear benefits to international migration, yet growth in migration flows has not been nearly as dramatic as the growth in trade and capital flows. On a global basis, international migration has increased much more slowly, as figure 2-3 illustrates. Migrants composed 2 percent of the world population in 1960, a share that rose to only 3 percent by 2008. This is a shockingly low percentage, particularly in light of the revolutions in transportation and communication that have occurred since the last great age of migration. In the century after 1820, some 55 million Europeans migrated to the United States and the rest of the New World (Canada, Australia, and New Zealand). This corresponds to emigration rates of fifty per thousand people for some countries. For comparison, emigration rates of ten per thousand would be considered high today.[11]

Today's low rates of international migration pose a puzzle to economists. The gains from labor migration, particularly from poor to rich nations, are huge and persistent. Estimates suggest workers who migrate to the United States from developing countries earn more than four times as much as similar workers back in the source countries.[12] A worker who migrates to the United States from Mexico increases his income on the order of $10,000 to $16,000 annually even after adjusting for purchasing power differences.[13]

One measure of the gains from immigration is remittances, money sent by migrants to family members who remain in the home country. Due to the rise in migration and the fall in costs of remitting money home, remittances have kept pace with financial globalization more broadly, rising from $2 billion to $433 billion between 1970 and 2008.[14] Measured as a share of world GDP, remittances have increased from less than 0.1 percent to over 0.7 percent of total output during this time period (figure 2-3).[15] This money is a vital source of income not only for recipient families but also for many developing countries. Remittances are the second largest source, behind foreign direct investment, of external funds for developing countries overall.[16]

It thus appears that financial markets as well as markets for goods and services have achieved high levels of global integration, while labor markets have been on the sidelines. Indeed, labor flows are the last frontier in globalization. Given how large the economic benefits of migration are, why is the number of migrants so small? We know, of course, that individuals value much more than simply the money in their wallets, and money alone will not overcome the inherent reluctance to move that many people feel.[17] But as chapter 1 made clear, in the case of the United States, host-country policies play a role in suppressing migration flows and stymieing potential migrants. A government may restrict migration for a variety of reasons, from national security concerns to xenophobia. A common motivation is the fear that immigration will slow economic growth and reduce natives' standard of living. To gauge whether such fears are justified, we consider below the insights from research on the economic effects of immigration.

Economic Effects of Immigration

There is a voluminous literature on the economic effects of immigration, particularly on the effect on natives' wages. Although there is broad consensus among economists that immigration benefits an economy overall, this message has not always been conveyed effectively to policymakers. This section explores three key questions about the economic impact of immigration: First, what is the impact of immigration on the macroeconomy and on economic growth? Second, how do immigrant inflows affect native workers' wages and employment? Third, how does immigration affect government revenues and expenditures?

The immigration surplus. Immigration grows the economy in many different ways. By simply adding more workers, immigration makes the economy bigger. Immigration accounted for one-half of U.S. labor force growth during the last decade. The resultant increases in output and income accrue mostly to immigrants, but natives reap a modest income gain referred to as the "immigration surplus." Owners of capital—firms that employ workers, and their shareholders—benefit as well. The immigration surplus under conventional assumptions is estimated to be between 0.1 and 0.4 percent of GDP, or about $15 to $60 billion per year.[18]

There is an interesting fact about the immigration surplus: it is larger when the differences between natives and immigrants are larger. If immigrants are just clones of natives—if they have the same skill distribution and arrive with as much physical capital (wealth) as natives, on average—then the immigration surplus is zero. In other words, natives gain little economically from letting in people who are much like themselves. Immigration policies that engender this type of immigration are often motivated by other considerations, such as desire for racial and religious homogeneity or concerns about rising inequality and the pace of immigrant assimilation.

The fact that the immigration surplus is maximized when immigrants are most different from natives has clear implications for policy. An immigration policy based on family reunification will primarily admit people like those already here. A market-based immigration policy, in contrast, will attract types of human capital that are relatively scarce.

Immigration and economic growth. While illustrative of the gains from immigration, the immigration surplus is a simplistic calculation that does not incorporate the sustained growth effects of immigration. Long-run economic growth is driven by productivity growth; just adding more workers cannot sustain permanent increases in a nation's per capita income. But the evidence is mounting that immigration has a role to play in productivity growth. In fact, research indicates *high-skilled* immigration spurs technological progress by contributing to innovation. It does so through four channels: immigrants innovate, facilitate the transfer of technology, contribute to economies of scale, and increase innovative competition by reducing the power of vested interests and speeding up the process of creative destruction.[19]

There is ample empirical evidence of the first channel in the United States. Research indicates that high-skilled immigrants boost innovation and have a significant impact on research and development. Not only do they raise innovation directly, as measured by the number of patents issued to the foreign born, but they boost total patent activity by natives as well.[20] Immigrants also create new businesses at higher rates than natives.[21] Immigrant entrepreneurship is particularly high in science and engineering; in fact, 25 percent of high-tech startups between 1995 and 2005 had at least one key foreign-born founder.[22]

Immigrants are more entrepreneurial than natives for several different reasons, but an important factor is positive selection. Foreigners are not picked at random to move to the United States. They come of their own accord. The factors that influence them to migrate suggest they are positively selected out of their home populations, either in terms of earnings, education, health, ability, or willingness to take risk.[23]

The second channel is technology transfer. Immigrant inflows are a critical source of workers for science and technology industries in the United States. Some of these workers bring skills and new knowledge from abroad, while others disseminate technological knowledge when they return home.[24] Immigrants made up 38 percent of employment growth in the science, technology, engineering, and mathematics (STEM) workforce in the United States during the period 1994–2002.[25] The foreign born accounted for 57 percent of employment growth in STEM occupations during 2003–2008.[26] These numbers would likely have been higher absent the numerical limits on skilled worker visas discussed in chapter 1.

The ability to hire immigrants in R&D-intensive industries has contributed to the growth of high-tech clusters, such as Silicon Valley and Route 128.[27] These clusters have positive growth spillovers because they exploit a form of economies of scale, the third channel through which immigration spurs technological progress. Producers are grouped together, and so are their suppliers and workers. This allows firms easier access to their factor inputs (labor, intermediate goods, and capital markets), which in turn allows for a competitive, dynamic environment with more innovation and lower input costs.[28] Interestingly, economists have discovered that agglomeration economies are not specific to production clusters but arise more generally when cities have high concentrations of highly educated workers. In fact, cities with high concentrations (over 25 percent) of college-educated adults grew more than three times as fast between 1980 and 2000 as cities with high concentrations of less-educated workers.[29] Skills drove growth by boosting innovation and productivity, which in turn allowed cities to better adapt to change. And, of course, many of those college graduates are foreign-born or are the children of immigrants.

One last contribution of high-skilled immigration to economic growth is its effect on institutions. The Austrian economist Joseph Schumpeter pioneered the idea that entrepreneurship and innovation change market structure by undermining existing businesses, individuals, and institutions.[30] Without this process of "creative destruction," incumbents will use their power to support anticompetitive practices and policies and stymie technological change. Research has documented that countries with institutions protecting vested interests have less technological progress and has also suggested that more international competition limits the power of vested interests to block innovation.[31] Some economists have argued more broadly that factor mobility, whether of capital or labor, shapes public policy in a way that is more conducive to efficiency and growth.[32] As long as people can move themselves or their wealth, there are limits to the policies that governments can adopt in favor of special interests.

What about low-skilled immigrants? The economic contributions of less-educated immigrants can be represented adequately with the standard notion of the immigration surplus. Low-skilled immigrants are not a key part of the innovative processes described above; their impact on long-run productivity growth in the host country is unlikely to be significant. This type of immigration still has important economic benefits, however, that are similar to the gains from trade. As with trade, even though natives reap a net gain, there are winners and losers, as we discuss below. The gains from immigration stem from the fact that native and foreign-born workers can specialize in activities according to their comparative advantage—jobs for which they each have a low opportunity cost. As a result, more output can be produced with fewer resources and economic activity rises while prices fall. Low-skilled immigration in particular lowers the prices of labor-intensive goods and services.

The price effects of immigration also affect natives' choice of activity. Research suggests, for example, that low-skilled female migration has significantly lowered the cost of child care over the last three decades. This has led in turn to higher labor force participation and fertility among highly educated native-born women.[33]

Access to low-skilled labor makes a difference to firms, although it matters to some more than to others. Fruit and vegetable growers and the construction sector, for example, are heavily reliant on low-skilled migrant labor, particularly seasonal labor. Certain manufacturing industries that face tough international competition, such as textiles and apparel, also are highly dependent on migrant workers to keep their costs down. Immigration supporters argue that these producers need access to migrant labor, while immigration critics argue that the absence of cheap labor would force these firms to adopt labor-saving technologies and that the United States could simply import these goods if U.S. labor costs rise.[34] The truth is probably somewhere in between; some small, high-cost producers would go out of business without access to foreign labor, while big, low-cost companies could afford to adopt new technologies. Some goods would be imported, while others—particularly services—would not. It is clear that with less immigration by low-skilled workers, consumers would pay higher prices than they do now, particularly in the short run, and imports would likely rise.

There are a number of additional benefits from the influx of foreign workers. Immigrants are consumers as well as workers, and they have demand-side effects, too. For example, immigrants have driven up house prices and rents in U.S. cities, helping revitalize inner-city neighborhoods and halt or slow the pace of urban decline that was prevalent in the 1970s and 1980s.[35] Positive demand effects that boost prices may also raise natives' wages. One study found that the 1980 Mariel boatlift, which brought 125,000 Cubans into Miami over a five-month period, boosted retail sales extensively and actually raised natives' wages.[36]

Another economic benefit of migration overall, particularly of low-skilled (often illegal) immigration, is the responsiveness of foreign-born workers to variation in labor demand both over time and across regions. Immigrants, particularly less-educated unauthorized immigrants, are more responsive than natives to the business cycle. They are willing to move across sectors and states and even to return home or not come at all.[37] This greater mobility reduces unemployment rates, mitigates the cyclicality of government revenues and expenditures, and helps the economy run more efficiently.

Labor market effects of immigration. Theory suggests there are winners and losers from immigration, particularly in the short run. Yet despite the sizable flow of immigrants into the United States, the bulk of research indicates that immigration has had relatively little effect on most natives' labor market outcomes. In its comprehensive 1997 study, the National Research Council concluded that immigration has had only a small adverse impact on competing groups of native workers.[38]

Immigration to the United States has had a more adverse effect on low-skilled natives than on high-skilled natives. This is both because the numbers of low-skilled immigrants is so large and because these immigrants are more substitutable for natives in jobs that do not require much formal education or English fluency.[39] Two things bear pointing out, however. First, low-skilled natives' wages have been falling since the 1970s for a host of reasons unrelated to immigration, including the rising skill premium, declining unionization rate, and falling real minimum wage.[40] Second, it is earlier immigrants, not natives, who experience the most negative impact of immigrant inflows on their labor market outcomes.[41]

Given that over a million foreign-born workers enter the United States every year, one might expect larger and more negative wage effects than the empirical evidence suggests. There are several theories that can explain why immigration does not appear to harm most natives. Immigrants concentrate in areas and occupations that are experiencing growth and can better absorb new entrants. The industry mix may change, or industries may utilize labor more intensively, in response to immigrant inflows. For example, a garment industry still exists in Los Angeles because of the large numbers of immigrants there, and households hire more help with cleaning, child rearing and lawn care than they would absent immigration.

Supply also creates its own demand, with immigrants buying goods and services from each other as well as from natives. Immigration's effect on aggregate demand can actually push natives' wages up, further mitigating any downward pressure from increased labor market competition.[42] Natives may move away from areas experiencing large influxes of immigrants, spreading out any effects across the country and making them harder to measure. Finally, in the long run, the capital stock should fully adjust to the influx of labor, in which case immigration does not adversely affect average wages.[43]

One important way in which immigration affects labor markets is to exacerbate income inequality. Because immigrants are concentrated in low-education, low-skilled jobs, any adverse income effects are greatest on competing native workers. At the same time, low-skilled—and perhaps even high-skilled—immigrant workers are a complement to well-educated, high-skilled native workers. Immigration thus may boost income inequality by lowering the incomes of natives at the bottom of the distribution while potentially raising them at the upper end. Immigration also changes the composition of the population—immigrants comprise an increasing proportion of the left tail of the income distribution. Because immigrants are poorer, on average, than U.S. natives, simply having more immigrants tends to increase income inequality by some measures. Immigration thus appears to have been one of the factors that has contributed to the rise in income inequality experienced in the United States since the 1970s.[44]

Immigration probably has had a bigger effect on inequality in living standards. While all consumers benefit from the lower-priced goods and services produced by immigrants, middle- and upper-class households tend to consume more of these products, particularly labor-intensive household services. As noted above, the effect of immigration on child care prices has raised labor force participation among highly educated native-born women, thereby boosting incomes and living standards for households at the top end of the distribution.

The fiscal impact of immigration. The fiscal costs of immigration are important because there is no flipside to higher taxes. With labor market effects, we know that lower wages mean lower prices and that consumers benefit on average from the immigration surplus. However, if immigration increases the tax burden, there are few tangible offsets for taxpayers to console themselves with, at least in the short run. Research on the fiscal impact of contemporaneous immigrant inflows is less encouraging than estimates of other economic effects.[45]

Like natives, immigrants' net fiscal contributions are a function of their income. Because immigrants tend to be poorer than natives, they also tend to pay less in taxes and—when legal—to be more likely to qualify for welfare programs than natives. Immigrant-headed households qualify for welfare at greater rates not because they are single-parent families or because the adults are not working. On the contrary, many immigrant-headed households are poor because they have low wages, no health insurance, and more children than is the norm for native-born households. Immigrants' U.S.-born children are eligible for government assistance programs on the same terms as all other natives, regardless of their parents' legal status.[46] Relatively high fertility rates among immigrants put significant pressures on school systems in areas with large numbers of immigrants, while low rates of health insurance coverage in this population burden public health-care providers.

The net federal impact of current immigrants appears to be small, but state and local governments in areas with large populations of low-wage immigrants experience a sizable negative fiscal impact. Although recent comprehensive analysis of immigration's fiscal impact is hard to come by, a 1997 study by the National Research Council concluded that the net present value of the average fiscal impact of an immigrant over his lifetime was –$89,000 for an immigrant with less than a high school education and +$105,000 for an immigrant with more than a high school education.[47] The average fiscal impact of immigration masks large differences across states. Due to generous welfare programs and a large low-income immigrant population, Californians bear by far the greatest tax burden as a result of immigration. For example, in 1994–1995 each native-headed household in California paid an additional $1,178 in taxes as a result of immigration.[48] Interestingly, while there are few reliable estimates of the fiscal cost of unauthorized immigrants, they likely cost less than low-skilled legal immigrants because they are eligible for fewer public programs.[49]

Once the fiscal costs are subtracted from the economic gains to immigration, the overall gains to natives from immigration are close to zero.[50] Under conventional assumptions, it turns out that the fiscal costs are about equal to the economic gains, at about 0.2 percent of GDP each.[51] We draw one important conclusion from this naive calculation: the overall effect is neutral only because high-skilled immigrants greatly defray the costs imposed by low-skilled immigrants. The fiscal costs of immigration therefore can be reduced and the economic gains increased by raising the share of high-skilled immigrants in the flow. The other option, cutting taxes by reducing large expenditure items, such as schooling and health services for immigrants and their children, is not a viable option since it would slow immigrants' economic and cultural integration and reduce their economic and fiscal contributions in the long run.

There are several shortcomings with this back-of-the-envelope calculation. First, it does not take into account the dynamic effects of high-skilled immigration on economic growth discussed above. Second, the fiscal cost of immigration changes under a longer time horizon. As immigrants assimilate, their incomes and tax payments grow. And since their children, grandchildren, and successive generations more closely resemble natives, the fiscal gains (or costs) from immigration tend to disappear over the very long run.

Immigration Policies: A Global Perspective

The economic and fiscal effects of immigration provide the underpinnings for recent immigration policy reforms both in the United States and abroad. In the last decade or two, developed nations have been increasing their barriers to low-skilled immigration but scrambling to create programs that attract high-skilled foreign workers or retain foreign graduates of host-country universities (see box 2-2). Despite such programs, the United States continues to have several important advantages in attracting and retaining high-skilled immigrants. Lower taxes and greater earnings inequality mean that returns to skill and thus earnings tend to be higher in the United States than in other developed countries. The United States also has a more flexible labor market and a smaller safety net than most developed economies, which results in higher employment rates. While many European countries may welcome high-skilled migrants to work on a temporary basis, the United States offers a path to permanent residence and naturalized citizenship for many such immigrants. Still, the relative competitiveness of the United States on the global labor market is likely suffering as other destinations become more accessible. Certainly this appears to be the case with regard to education. The share of foreign tertiary (university) students worldwide who study in the United States fell from 25 percent in 2000 to 20 percent in 2007.[52]

Box 2-2: Programs Aimed at Attracting High-Skilled Immigrants in Other Countries

Developed countries are increasingly competing for high-skilled workers.[53] Since 2006, France, Germany, the Netherlands, and the United Kingdom all changed their immigration policies in an effort to attract high-skilled workers. France, for example, gives precedence to labor migrants who satisfy particular skill needs. The United Kingdom has a points system that specifically targets high-skilled individuals. Highly skilled workers need not even have a specific job offer as long as they can demonstrate sufficient English ability, meet an asset requirement, and meet a points threshold based on age, education, and earnings. Having an MBA from a program listed as one of the top fifty in the world is sufficient to meet the points threshold. The EU is moving on this issue as well and, in May 2009, the Council of the European Union adopted a directive to bring in temporary high-skilled workers under the Blue Card program. Member states (except Denmark, Ireland, and the United Kingdom) will have two years to incorporate the law into domestic legislation.

Countries are also encouraging foreign students to remain after graduation. The United Kingdom allows students to remain for up to twelve months to search for a job after graduating from an approved institution of higher education. Finland and Ireland allow university graduates to remain for several months to job-search as well. In Germany, employers who hire foreign graduates of German universities are exempt from labor market testing if the graduate is employed in the field of study.

In international comparisons it becomes immediately obvious that the United States puts far less emphasis not only on skilled workers but on workers in general than other developed nations. The composition of immigrants across admission categories is considerably different in the United States than in other nations belonging to the Organisation for Economic Co-operation and Development (OECD) (see table 2-1). The United States is not the outlier in admitting humanitarian migrants, but it certainly favors family-based migrants and disfavors work-based migrants more than any other nation listed.

Interestingly, there is no international framework analogous to the WTO that promotes and governs the international movement of people on a global level.[54] Faced with the lack of a multilateral framework for migration, developed nations may have agreements with each other, but they typically do not engage in meaningful bilateral migration agreements with developing countries.[55] Notable exceptions are Spain, which has several bilateral migration agreements with other nations, and the Philippines, which manages temporary migration agreements with a number of countries through its Overseas Employment Office. Immigration policy does not lend itself to multilateral agreements because it is inherently asymmetric: people flows are generally in one direction. Unless the negotiations involve some type of forced return migration—as the *bracero* program did—sending and receiving governments may not have much to discuss.

While industrial nations tend to shy away from labor migration agreements with developing countries, they have a range of agreements with like countries. The EU-15 nations, for example, extend free movement to each other, although most elected not to extend free movement rights to the poorer central and eastern European nations that joined the EU following enlargement in 2004 and 2007.[56] The exceptions were the United Kingdom, Ireland, and Sweden, which granted free movement to the 2004 accession countries. No existing EU nation extended free movement to Romania and Bulgaria when they joined the EU in 2007. The NAFTA countries also treat labor mobility asymmetrically. The United States, for example, allows unlimited temporary migration of high-skilled workers in specialty occupations from Canada and Mexico but makes no similar allowance for less-educated workers.[57] Australia and Canada use immigration point systems to discourage low-skilled immigration.

TABLE 2-1
COMPOSITION OF LEGAL PERMANENT IMMIGRANT INFLOWS IN 2006

Country	Total Number (thousands)	Work (%)	Family (%)	Humani- tarian (%)	Other (%)
Australia	191.9	40.7	51.1	7.4	0.9
Austria	46.4	47.7	41.0	11.1	0.3
Belgium	36.1	58.0	35.4	6.6	0
Canada	251.6	22.1	60.8	17.0	0.1
Denmark	21.7	65.7	23.8	5.0	5.5
Finland	13.9	47.8	35.9	12.4	3.9
France	169.0	26.1	59.0	4.4	10.5
Germany	216.0	70.3	23.3	2.8	3.6
Italy	204.3	53.2	41.7	3.1	2.0
Japan	96.1	29.8	31.3	0.1	38.8
Netherlands	59.4	29.0	46.6	24.3	0
New Zealand	54.8	32.6	57.9	9.6	0
Norway	28.0	38.0	50.0	12.0	0
Portugal	25.1	37.5	62.1	0	0.4
Sweden	74.0	35.0	37.1	27.9	0
Switzerland	86.3	71.8	20.9	5.0	2.4
United Kingdom	343.2	53.2	31.8	8.9	6.0
United States	1,266.3	5.6	70.3	17.1	7.0

SOURCE: OECD, International Migration Outlook 2008.
NOTE: Work includes free movement migrants; humanitarian is refugees and asylees.

In some countries, such as the United Arab Emirates, Kuwait, Singapore, and Saudi Arabia, government policy allows for the importation of low-skilled workers but under very strict conditions. Workers, particularly private household workers, often have limited rights and are not protected by employment laws that apply to native workers. These workers are frequently not allowed to bring their families or become permanent residents. Authoritarian governments have greater success with such migration policies and temporary work contracts because they can go to extreme lengths to enforce the law.

Authoritarian governments are also able to pass more draconian legislation to begin with. In democracies, legislation has to enjoy public support in order to pass and become law. The repeated failure of the U.S. Congress to pass comprehensive immigration reform legislation in recent years holds several lessons for future proposed reforms. To succeed, a bill must satisfy three key constituencies: employers who hire immigrants, workers who compete with immigrants, and consumers. Employers generally want greater numbers of high-skilled immigrants, a path to legalization for current unauthorized immigrants, and either a guest-worker program or other means of ensuring continued streams of low-skilled foreign workers. Other voters, in contrast, tend to be concerned about border security and want to stem the flow of illegal immigration. Voters' preferences regarding the magnitude and composition of legal inflows tend to reflect their experiences with labor market and fiscal impacts; well-educated natives are more likely to oppose high levels of immigration if they live in states with large numbers of immigrants and generous public assistance programs, for example, while low-skilled natives are concerned about labor market competition from immigrants.[58]

The priorities of these three constituencies obviously conflict. Employers benefit from bigger immigration inflows, which puts downward pressure on wages. Workers want smaller inflows of competing workers in order to boost their own wages. Consumers recognize that they benefit from larger immigrant inflows, since more workers means lower prices. Still, consumers do not want to pay significantly higher taxes to provide such immigrants with public services.

How can policy best address these seemingly conflicting objectives? It can emphasize employment-based migration, as desired by employers, while providing mechanisms to shield natives from adverse labor market and fiscal effects. Adverse labor-market effects would likely be smaller if immigration emphasized employment-based migration rather than family reunification. Workers in shortest supply would enter and be hired in the fastest-growing regions and industries. Prioritizing high-skilled labor migration over low-skilled family reunification migration also would change immigration's effect on budgets at the federal, state, and local levels. In the rest of this chapter, we make the case for employment-based immigration as the primary goal of immigration policy reform. We outline five additional goals meant to address the efficiency, flexibility, viability, and comprehensiveness of reform.

Goal 1: Prioritize Employment-Based Migration

The first goal of immigration reform should be to turn the table on the priorities of U.S. immigration policy and put employment-based immigration first. Job-based immigration not only brings in the workers the U.S. economy requires; it also brings in immigrants with needed skills, a strong work ethic, and the desire to succeed. Employment-based immigration is the best way to confront a host of problems facing the United States, including a slowing pace of technological progress, declining competitiveness, changing demographics, increased offshoring, and the growing health care needs of an aging population.

Increase high-skilled worker migration. For decades, the United States was the premier destination for the world's high-skilled workers. In this new era of globalization, the race for talent is heating up as other Western nations compete with the United States to attract high-skilled immigrants (see box 2-2). The labor mobility already in place in much of the EU, with more to come in the future, gives European nations an advantage over the United States in attracting and retaining European talent. In addition, Canada and Australia attract high-skilled immigrants who cannot enter the United States due to lengthy queues for employment-based green cards and the caps on H-1B temporary work visas.

The United States needs to redesign its immigration policy in order to compete with other nations in attracting high-skilled workers. The country faces critical skill shortages in areas where it has a comparative advantage, such as information technology, medicine, research and development, engineering, and higher education.[59] Retaining the country's comparative advantage in these high-value-added fields requires aggressively pursuing the best and brightest both at home and abroad. Increasingly, however, the best in science, math, and medicine are found abroad.[60] The United States has a number of strengths that appeal to such workers, including relatively low taxes and high wages. Immigration policy reform should capitalize on these assets.

Reform needs to reach all the way down to student visas. Graduate students are increasingly bypassing U.S. universities for schools in the United Kingdom, Australia, France, and other places where graduate instruction is offered in English.[61] The United States makes it difficult for foreign students to enter because of concerns that they will stay. This is a sign of how wrongheaded U.S. policy is: many of these students are the very people immigration policy *should* aim to admit.

Immigration reform also needs to encompass what happens after foreign students graduate. About one-half of recent U.S. doctorates in science and engineering were awarded to foreign students.[62] Relaxing the caps on employment-based migration in order to allow these students to remain here is crucial to future U.S. technological advancement and productivity growth. For years, foreign graduates of U.S. colleges and universities have been the backbone of employment-based high-skilled migration. Any reform should prop this door open further rather than slam it closed.[63]

Increasing high-skilled immigration would have the added benefit of keeping more high-paying jobs in the United States. Some of the jobs done by high-skilled workers, such as computer programming and contract writing, have already been moved overseas. It is higher productivity that currently keeps most of these potentially mobile jobs here. But technological change and rising education levels in other countries may well make it more cost-effective for companies to offshore such work in the future. Immigration policy alone cannot stop such a trend. But encouraging firms to hire the foreign-born in the United States instead of in their home countries by raising caps on employment-based immigration will lower pressures to move jobs offshore.

Allocate work visas to low-skilled workers, too. Prioritizing employment-based immigration does not mean at the cost of low-skilled immigration. On the contrary, a goal of immigration reform should be to provide legal means for low-skilled workers to be admitted. There are two reasons for this. First, there are jobs for them to fill, as recent decades' experience has amply shown. Second, providing legal means of immigrating helps reduce illegal immigration. Low-skilled foreign-born workers fill important niches in the U.S. job market and generate significant consumer surplus. The Bureau of Labor Statistics projects that three-quarters of all new jobs over the next ten years will *not* require a bachelor's degree.[64] Meanwhile, the native-born supply of low-skilled workers is falling as older workers retire and young workers are increasingly likely to have at least some college education. A more educated native population and inflows of high-skilled immigrants create greater demand for services provided by low-skilled workers, such as construction, child care, landscaping, and food services. Many of these services cannot be imported or automated and offer limited possibilities for productivity improvements. Trade can lower prices for traded goods, but not for most of the service industry. Bringing in low-skilled workers to fill these jobs enables natives to work in higher-value-added jobs and increases real incomes by keeping the prices of labor-intensive goods and services low.[65]

The aging of the U.S. workforce will remove over fifty million workers from the labor force during the next twenty years.[66] This demographic change will mean more vacancies, especially in health care and related industries, which already lack sufficient workers, both high- and low-skilled.[67] Immigration policy should allow employers to bring in workers to meet shortages in health care—not just high-skilled workers such as doctors and nurses, but also health care aides.

A new policy that seeks to bring in high-skilled workers instead of unifying families would cause legal immigration of low-skilled workers to slow. It is thus important for comprehensive immigration reform to ensure an adequate inflow of low-skilled workers via employment-based visas. The United States has a comparative advantage in high-skilled jobs, but some low-skilled jobs will always remain. The overall gains for the economy are greatest if the United States allows foreign workers to fill some of the low-skilled jobs and provides natives with incentives to increase their own skill levels. Just as the gains from free trade can be used to compensate those who lose the most from trade liberalization, gains from immigration can be redistributed to natives who are harmed by immigration; this point is discussed further under goal 4 below.

Given the high demand for low-skilled workers, the falling number of less-educated natives, and the United States' geographical proximity to millions of willing workers in nations like Mexico, the failure to allocate visas to low-skilled labor would inevitably result in continued large-scale illegal immigration. At least in the short run, the United States needs to continue to accommodate relatively large numbers of low-skilled foreign workers in order to minimize labor and product market disruptions; admitting these workers legally is better than continuing to countenance large-scale illegal entry and unauthorized work.

Goal 2: Set Flexible Caps That Increase with Economic Growth

Instead of micromanaging myriad types of visas and imposing nonsensical caps, the federal government should set flexible caps on employment-based immigration that reflect both short- and long-run changes in supply and demand. The number of visas available in a given year should increase with the underlying long-term trend in the growth rate of real GDP, but should also fluctuate in response to the business cycle (as captured by changes in unemployment, for example).

Allowing immigrant admissions to depend on demand—in other words, allowing U.S. employers to recruit more foreign workers when U.S. labor markets tighten—would promote economic growth. Under current policy, employers are unable to bring in more workers in response to shortages if immigration quotas are already met. Meanwhile, immigrants can (and do) enter under family-sponsored preferences even if labor markets are slack and employers are not hiring. Unlike a policy based on employer sponsorship, current policy exacerbates swings in the business cycle rather than smoothing them.

Immigration reformers should consider the supply side as well when setting caps. The supply of immigrants depends on economic conditions in the home country, ties to relatives already in the United States, costs of migrating, and perceived economic gains to migration. Hurricanes in Central America or an economic downturn in Mexico or elsewhere can result in more U.S. immigration even if U.S. demand for foreign workers is unchanged. In the past, failure to raise the number of legal immigrants admitted in response to economic crises abroad has resulted in surges in illegal immigration that had to be accommodated after the fact. Cutting off that channel via interior and border enforcement is important, but so is providing legal alternatives. The federal government can also influence supply and demand by changing the cost of migration in response to economic forces both at home and abroad, a strategy discussed more fully in chapter 3.

Goal 3: Encourage Short-Term Migration

Much of current immigration policy was designed with the view that immigration should be permanent and all immigrants should eventually become

U.S. citizens. To this day, green card holders who leave the country for more than twelve months can be stripped of their permanent resident visa. Non-immigrants who travel on H-1B, TN, or other temporary visas often fear they will not be allowed back into the United States. Consular officers and Border Patrol agents have broad powers to determine whether foreigners requesting admission have violated or will violate visa terms and conditions.

Such policies are outdated in a new era of globalization. Mobility is rising, particularly among high-skilled workers, and there are great rewards to working overseas. Even Americans are living and working abroad in record numbers. Migration flows will only continue to swell, given the tremendous disparities in standards of living within and across countries, falling transportation costs, and improved information about opportunities elsewhere. Moreover, as the economic center of gravity moves away from the United States and Western Europe toward Asia, the need for flexible travel and immigration policies in the West grows more urgent each day. A new policy emphasizing employment-based immigration over family reunification needs to recognize, and accept, that return migration or circular migration is likely to increase. These short sojourns should not be viewed with suspicion but rather seen as a positive development and a necessary step toward increasing U.S. competitiveness globally.

The assumption that all immigrants want to remain permanently ignores the realities of U.S. immigration. Estimates suggest return migration rates at the turn of the last century were as high as 50 percent for immigrants from some European countries and averaged about 30 percent overall.[68] While many early immigrants did stay permanently, the dangers and high costs of travel may have played a greater role than true desire in the decision to remain. As transportation costs fell, many immigrants were "birds of passage" who came to fill U.S. demand for workers, accumulate savings, and then return home.[69] Even today, many immigrants return home when they have saved enough money to start a business, pay a debt, buy a home, or retire. Estimates suggest that about 20 percent of immigrants in the United States do not stay permanently, either because they return home or migrate to another country.[70] As many as one-half of H-1B workers depart.[71]

Given that return migration is common, and that even so-called permanent immigration is often not really permanent, the distinction between permanent and temporary immigration in the current immigration system should be relaxed. The United States has taken a step in the right direction by no longer requiring holders of H-1B and some other visas to attest to "nonimmigrant intent"—that is, these visa holders do not need to declare that they intend to eventually return to their home country.[72] However, the nonimmigrant intent rule remains in force for many business, student, and work visas and can cause problems later on if the person holding such a visa decides he wants to stay permanently in the United States.

Return migration and cyclical migration offer several benefits for the United States. Return migration and cyclical migration by low-skilled immigrants reduce the long-run fiscal burden associated with immigration discussed earlier in this chapter. For low- and high-skilled immigrants, the decision to migrate only temporarily means they are less likely to bring their families with them, reducing fiscal costs at the state and local level. While return migration of high-skilled immigrants offers fewer direct economic benefits to the United States, it can promote international trade, stimulate technology transfer, and improve foreign relations.

Encouraging return migration is also in the interest of the home country. Developing countries in particular stand to gain from return migration of high-skilled migrants. Silicon Valley and its networks of Chinese, Indian, Israeli, and Taiwanese immigrants and return migrants is a canonical example.[73] Such "brain circulation" can boost the rate of growth in home countries, encourage capital flows and technology transfer, reduce international inequalities, and spur institutional change. Return of relatively low-skilled migrants can also bring benefits for home countries, since migrants repatriate with skills or savings acquired in the United States. Even while immigrants are present in the United States, home countries benefit, since immigrants who plan to return home tend to send back higher remittances than those who plan to stay.[74]

Goal 4: Mitigate Negative Labor Market Impacts

Although discussions of immigration reform inevitably confront the issue of possible adverse labor-market effects, it is worth asking whether protecting American workers from competition should be a goal of immigration policy.

A policy designed solely to minimize adverse effects on natives' earnings or employment prospects would be akin to protectionist trade policies that insulate U.S. industry from foreign competition. Competition and market forces are what ultimately guarantee the United States' economic strength and confer the greatest welfare gains on future generations. Like international trade, immigration has positive spillovers on the broader economy; it lowers prices, raises profits, and spurs innovation. Focusing on negative wage impacts among narrow groups of workers ignores gains to the economy as a whole.

Nonetheless, it is important to address concerns about the effect of immigration on natives' wage and employment outcomes, since these are among the main impediments to immigration policy reform. The United States currently tries to limit adverse labor-market effects via labor market testing for employment-based immigrants.[75] This process requires that the Bureau of Labor Statistics certify that there are no U.S. workers able, willing, qualified, and available to accept, at the prevailing wage, the job that the foreign worker will fill, and that employment of the foreign worker will not adversely affect the wages and working conditions of similarly employed U.S. workers. Labor market testing costs both money and time yet achieves very little, if anything. In a labor force of over 155 million workers, it is sheer folly to try to measure the wage or employment impact of bringing in one more individual. Predictably, few applications are denied.[76]

There are better, less costly ways to address concerns about adverse labor-market impacts. After all, the two main ways in which low-skilled immigrants enter the United States—illegal immigration and family-sponsored immigration—completely bypass the formal labor-market testing process.[77] It would be more effective to crack down on illegal immigration via interior enforcement and to switch the emphasis from family reunification to employment as the main basis for immigration. As employment becomes the central focus of immigration policy, the government can protect native workers by taxing foreign labor. Charging fees to employers who want to hire foreign workers will discourage their use if other workers are available and will generate revenue when other workers are not. Adopting a system that changes the number of immigrants admitted in response to economic conditions would also help cushion the labor market impact of immigration. Finally, the fees paid by immigrants' employers could fund retraining programs for natives displaced by foreign workers, much as the

Trade Adjustment Assistance program does for workers adversely affected by international trade. Such programs would make the U.S. workforce more skilled and more flexible, necessary characteristics in this era of globalization. Details on all of these proposals are in the next chapter.

Goal 5: Limit Adverse Fiscal Impacts

A primary concern regarding immigration of low-skilled individuals is that their low tax payments are not enough to cover the increased expenses the government bears in conjunction with their migration, settlement, and family formation. Estimates suggest that, for an immigrant with less than a high school education, the average net present value of the fiscal impact is negative in both the short and long run. Meanwhile, fiscal impacts are positive and large for immigrants with a high school education or more.[78]

The current immigration system appears designed to aggravate the fiscal impact of immigration by prioritizing green cards for extended families rather than workers. The fiscal costs of immigrants who are low-skilled, have many children, or arrive at older ages are very large. Money spent on schooling and health care for immigrant children is money well spent—this investment will pay off for the individual and U.S. society in the future in terms of faster assimilation, higher earnings, and a smaller fiscal burden. However, this is not the case for public funds spent on older immigrants, such as those entering as parents of U.S. citizens. These older immigrants are less likely to work and more likely to lack private health insurance than other legal permanent residents.[79] Many will not work the ten-year period required to qualify for Social Security and Medicare but will be poor enough to be eligible for Supplemental Security Income (SSI) and Medicaid in their old age. While estimates are hard to come by, family reunification, particularly if it involves elderly parents, is costly for U.S. taxpayers. The humane solution is not to cut off elderly immigrants who are already here, but rather to reduce the future inflow.

Immigration policy reform should also address the imbalance in how the fiscal costs of immigration are distributed. Currently, many of the costs are borne at the state and local levels, while the gains from payroll taxes accrue mainly at the federal level. The federal government needs to redistribute more funds to high-immigration states and localities to alleviate the fiscal burden on those areas. Facilitating short-term migration by bringing foreigners in on provisional rather than permanent visas would also improve the fiscal impact associated with immigration if low-skilled immigrants who currently settle permanently in the United States instead choose to seasonally migrate or return home at some point, reducing their reliance on government transfer programs.

Goal 6: End Illegal Immigration

Illegal immigration accounted for nearly one-half of net foreign-born inflows between 1990 and 2005.[80] Inflows this large cannot be ignored. Immigration reform must encompass a plan to deal with the undocumented population already here and to minimize future unauthorized immigration. Any new policy must address the illegal immigrant population because, in the interests of efficiency and equity, the new rules should apply to all. Additionally, if voters are going to support reform, they need to have reason to believe that laws will be enforced this time around.

Currently, immigration laws are not enforced consistently, and undocumented labor is allowed in and often left untaxed. Unauthorized workers and their employers therefore have an advantage over native and legal immigrant workers in the low-wage labor market. The benefits accrue largely to employers, who may be able to pay unauthorized immigrants lower wages than legal workers would make, and to consumers who benefit to the extent that lower costs get passed on in the form of lower prices. Hiring unauthorized workers may translate into lower costs for employers if they do not pay payroll and unemployment insurance taxes or spend less on fringe benefits, such as a health insurance or retirement plan.

Illegal status harms the immigrants themselves as well as competing workers and taxpayers. Unauthorized immigrants have little recourse if they are underpaid or otherwise mistreated by an employer. Undocumented workers who pay into Social Security are not accruing credit toward Social Security benefits and cannot claim unemployment or disability benefits if they lose their job or become disabled. Without a valid Social Security number, they cannot take advantage of benefits that many large employers offer, such as a 401(k) or similar defined contribution program. In most states unauthorized immigrants cannot get a driver's license and insurance. Everything from opening a bank account to enrolling in school or owning a business becomes difficult. And, because they carry cash around, they become victims of crime.

The problems that come from institutionalizing illegal immigration, as the United States has done over the last thirty years, are deep-rooted and long-lasting. It is time to forge a better way. As we suggest in chapter 3, it is unrealistic to believe that the United States can end all illegal immigration and unauthorized work, but it certainly can cost-effectively reduce the numbers well below current levels through a combination of work visas for low-skilled workers and stricter employment verification.

Conclusion

Liberalizing labor markets across borders may be the last frontier of globalization. The global economic gains from doing so are enormous, far outstripping those from further liberalization of trade in goods and services. But the distribution of gains in destination countries like the United States is problematic, as immigration creates winners and losers. Without a global structure to regulate immigration flows, countries can and do design their immigration policies to further strategic and economic interests, which increasingly lie in attracting scarce talent. U.S. immigration policy has not pursued these interests—indeed, it has remained largely unchanged for two decades except for stepped-up border enforcement. Other nations have developed new programs aimed at recruiting high-skilled immigrants. The United States risks losing the global competition for these workers if it does not reform its immigration policy.

This chapter presented goals for policy reform that fall into two broad categories. The first two goals are designed to promote economic growth and reduce inefficiencies in the immigration system. They aim to secure the nation's future prosperity by bringing in the best and brightest from around the world, by making immigration conditional on work, and by creating laws that are responsive to market conditions. The other four goals are designed to help shore up support for immigration reform among natives.

Since immigrants themselves are the biggest beneficiaries of immigration, immigration policy reform is possible only if some of those gains are transferred to natives, or if natives are shielded from adverse impacts of immigration. We propose charging employers fees for permits to hire foreign workers, which discourages the use of foreign labor; reducing the fiscal costs of immigration to help taxpayers; encouraging return migration; and minimizing illegal immigration by beefing up interior enforcement and by creating means for legal entry. These measures, discussed in detail in the next chapter, should help convince natives that the time is right for comprehensive immigration reform.

3

The Way: Market-Based Immigration Reform

This chapter explains how to redesign immigration policy in order to achieve the goals laid out in chapter 2. The discussion starts with a framework for handling future immigrant inflows, followed by a plan for treating existing immigrants, both legal and illegal. How to change the number and nature of future inflows is both the most difficult and the most important aspect of immigration reform. Inflows are vital to sustaining the long-run growth and competitiveness of the U.S. economy, because changing who *comes* to the United States will, over time, change who is *in* the United States.

By contrast, there is little that immigration policy can do to change the characteristics of the existing foreign-born population. Policy choices regarding this group therefore are largely limited to whether there should be a legalization scheme ("amnesty") for undocumented immigrants, and how best to alleviate green card queues among temporary workers who are trying to adjust status. We address these questions after we outline a policy for future immigration.

Provisional Immigration Based on Work

Plan: Immigration is predominately employment based, with most immigrants admitted provisionally, not permanently.

The plan proposed here admits people on the basis of work rather than family ties and makes a provisional five-year, renewable work visa the backbone of immigration policy. Numerical limits will apply to work visas, not green cards. Immigrants who wish to stay permanently will be able to earn permanent resident status over time on the basis of work and integration with U.S. society. Foreign-born spouses and minor children of U.S. citizens will be the only group granted permanent resident status without an initial provisional period.

Previous chapters explained why work-based immigration should be prioritized over family-based immigration. Work-based immigration will boost immigration's contribution to economic growth, result in better matches between the skills employers want and the skills that foreign workers have, and reduce adverse labor-market impacts and negative fiscal effects.

A provisional work visa, not a permanent one, is central to this policy. It offers the mobility and flexibility that are becoming more the norm and less the exception in the new era of globalization. It also makes sense to decide on permanent residence after a provisional period during which all parties involved acquire more information. Foreigners learn whether they want to stay and become permanent residents; employers learn about an immigrant's skill level and commitment; and the government can determine whether an immigrant has earned a green card based on his or her employment record and other information. In addition, this system eliminates the inefficient green card queues by limiting provisional work visas, not green cards.[1] There will be no queuing for provisional visas because they will be allocated in a spot market, as explained below.

This market will sell three types of provisional work-based permits: high-skilled, low-skilled, and seasonal. Employers must purchase a permit to hire a foreign worker; the type will depend on the position the worker will fill. Once hired, the foreign worker will receive a provisional work visa that allows him or her to legally enter the United States or to remain here in the case of a foreign student. There also will be provisional nonwork visas for dependents of provisional visa holders. Provisional visas will be renewable as long as a worker remains employed, although immigrants may eventually transition into permanent resident and, some time later, U.S. citizen status. The number of permits available to employers will be determined by the federal government based on demand-side forces in the U.S. labor market. The government will auction off these permits, and a resale market will be encouraged. We provide details on each component of the plan below.

Employers and Permits

Plan: To hire a foreign worker, employers must have either a high-skilled or low-skilled worker permit (valid for up to five years) or a seasonal worker permit (valid for less than one year).

Under our plan, employers who want to hire a foreign worker will have to purchase a permit either from the government, which will decide on the number of permits to issue during each allotted sales period, or on the resale market. Each permit will be valid for a fixed number of years. We suggest a five-year period for the high- and low-skilled visas. This is neither so short that it would discourage employers and workers from making firm-specific investments nor so long as to verge on being permanent. Seasonal visas will be valid for a much shorter period, perhaps less than a year. Employers without permits can hire foreigners who have adjusted to permanent resident status or who have naturalized and are U.S. citizens, but they may not hire foreign workers who have only provisional visas.[2]

The greatest benefit of this plan is that it allows employers to recruit foreign workers with the skills they demand. It allocates work visas to their highest valued use. Right now, over one million foreigners receive a green card each year, but they do not necessarily have the skills that employers seek. Employers who have been stymied by country or visa category caps will no longer be thwarted—the system will be much simpler, with caps on the total number of permits in just three broad categories. Employers have a choice of buying a new permit from the government or acquiring one from another firm. The price system of auctions and the resale market ensure that employers who want permits the most can acquire them.

In order to minimize the possibility of employer abuses and ensure an efficient allocation of labor, foreign workers on provisional visas need to be able to move between permitted employers. An employer who holds a permit may lose a foreign worker to a competitor who also holds a permit. In this case both employers would need to notify the government of the change. The employer who lost the worker could either fill the vacant slot with another foreign worker already in the country who has a provisional visa or bring over a new foreign worker. The former seems more likely than the latter, since screening provisional visa holders already in the country is easier than assessing the quality of potential workers overseas. If the employer no longer wants to employ a foreign worker with a provisional visa, the employer can sell the permit to another employer. Information about permit resales, such as the identities of buyers and sellers and the sales price, would need to be provided to the federal government in order to enforce the law and determine trends in labor demand.

It is important to make available both high- and low-skilled permits. If only a single type of permit were available, its price would likely be too high for an employer to profitably bring in a relatively low-skilled foreign worker even if U.S. workers were not available. Similarly, there should be a separate permit class for seasonal foreign workers. Those permits are for a much shorter duration than the permits for low- and high-skilled workers and hence would have a lower price.

There are two ways to distinguish between high- and low-skilled foreign workers: on the basis of job characteristics, or on the basis of earnings. For the first option, the federal government could create lists of high- and low-skilled occupations, and then employers would buy the appropriate permit for a given position. Alternatively, the government could set an earnings threshold below which a job is low-skilled and above which a job is high-skilled. The former plan would require random audits and penalties for violators, while compliance with the latter plan could be verified through tax documents. It also would be possible to distinguish between high- and low-skilled foreign workers on the basis of worker characteristics, such as education. This approach might be easier to implement, because the H-1B program currently has an educational credential requirement, and employers and migrants are used to that system. But it makes more sense to tie the skill level to the job rather than to the worker. This approach gives employers an incentive to find the most skilled worker available to fill a job, regardless of the worker's educational credentials.

Employers would be required to meet other provisions in order to hire foreign workers. First, benefit packages and tax withholding would have to be the same for provisional foreign workers, permanent immigrant workers, and native-born workers. The permit acts as a tax on foreign labor largely in order to discourage its use. If provisional foreign workers are not offered employer-provided benefits but permanent immigrants and natives are, then foreign labor is cheaper and the tax becomes less effective. The same is true if provisional foreign workers are exempted from Federal Insurance Contribution Act (FICA) taxes entirely or are later refunded their FICA contributions.[3] Employers could even be required to offer health insurance to the foreign worker and any accompanying dependents.

Second, employers will be required to electronically verify all workers' legal status. The proposed plan will fail if employers continue to hire unauthorized immigrants or hire provisional foreign workers without the requisite permit. Electronic verification of workers' and applicants' identities is therefore imperative, and biometric measures, such as fingerprints, probably will have to be included in order to cut down on identity theft and document fraud. The plan must include stiff penalties for employers who skirt the new rules. Strict work-site enforcement by the federal government is necessary to limit any competitive advantage gained by firms that cheat by hiring illegal immigrants.[4]

Like some current employment-based visas, the permit auctions can be structured to favor nonprofit or public institutions, such as universities and hospitals. Currently, these organizations are exempt from H-1B visa caps and from some of the H-1B fees. Because nonprofit and public institutions may not be able to shoulder the cost of the permits under the new system, the federal government could provide a rebate to these employers of all or part of the permit cost to enable them to hire professionals from abroad. It also could continue to allocate a set number of permits to such employers independent of the auction system.

Like the current employment-based system, the permit auctions will likely continue to favor foreign graduates of U.S. universities. Employers are better able to gauge the quality of these potential employees, on average, than people without any U.S. education and can interview them while they are attending U.S. schools before buying a permit to hire them. Workers who have studied in the United States are also likely to have better English skills than workers who have acquired all of their education abroad.

Domestic and foreign workers will both benefit from the new system. Domestic workers will benefit from the plan because it effectively imposes a tax on foreign workers. The permit requirement creates an employer preference for domestic workers by raising the cost of hiring foreign workers. (Another way to raise the costs of foreign labor would be to tax those workers directly, as discussed in box 3-1). At least some of the cost of permits will likely be passed on to foreign workers in the form of lower wages; there are no prevailing wage requirements in this plan. Currently, foreign workers on temporary work visas must receive at least the average wage paid to similar workers in that occupation and area.[5] Because foreign workers likely have relatively inelastic labor supply, meaning their willingness to work is not very sensitive to changes in wages, under our plan their earnings will absorb some or even most of the cost of the permit.[6]

Box 3-1: Why Not Tax Immigrant Earnings Directly?

An alternate way to raise the costs of foreign labor and generate revenue is to impose a higher income tax on immigrants or an additional payroll tax specific to immigrant workers.[7] A tax that is structured as a percentage of earnings or income has some advantages over the permit fee we propose. The government, and hence natives, would share in the gains when immigrants' incomes are high or rising. An income tax solves any cash-in-advance constraints employers purchasing permits might face, since the tax is paid while or after income is earned instead of in advance, as under the permit system. The tax easily could be progressive instead of proportional; high-wage immigrants could have a higher marginal tax rate than low-wage immigrants.[8]

However, higher taxes on labor earnings create bad incentives for individuals and distort the allocation of labor. Does it make sense to encourage foreigners to come and work in the United States, only to then discourage them from working hard by taxing them at higher rates than the rest of the population? A tax on immigrants' incomes also increases the incentive to work off the books. Just as an income tax can discourage an individual from working more hours, it also can distort an employer's decision about how to allocate labor on the margin. The flat permit fee is preferable because it does not affect marginal decision making, in contrast, and hence introduces fewer distortions. The permit fee is thus simpler to implement, and it avoids the adverse incentive effects and distortions of an immigrant income tax.[9]

Low-skilled workers will bear a relatively higher share of the permit cost than high-skilled workers—the more valuable and scarce a worker is, the better that worker's bargaining power. Many foreign workers therefore will have lower take-home pay than natives. On the margin, however, foreign workers will still be more expensive than similar native workers, and employers will not simply replace all their workers with "cheaper" foreign labor. In any case, the supply of foreign labor is capped by the number of permits. The permit will better protect U.S. workers than labor market testing does under the current system. And at the end of the day, the permit system essentially acts as a way of transferring some of the gains from migration from foreign workers to U.S. taxpayers.

The benefits to foreign workers are more obvious. The proposed plan allows more flexibility, makes changing jobs much easier, and allows workers to stay longer with less paperwork and uncertainty and without queuing. Eliminating country and category caps will enable many workers who otherwise were stuck in limbo for years to acquire permanent resident status as soon as they are eligible to do so.

Workers and Visas

Plan: A foreign worker receives a provisional visa to enter the United States when hired by an employer with a permit and after passing a background check. A visa holder can switch jobs as long as the new employer holds a permit and, after several years, can adjust to permanent resident status. Unemployed provisional visa holders must leave the United States after a grace period.

Foreign workers will receive a provisional visa to enter the United States if they are sponsored by an employer with a permit. The government will conduct a background check before admitting a specific individual, much as it currently does. The duration of the provisional visa will match the duration of the employer's permit and thus will be shorter for workers entering into seasonal jobs. These provisional visas are not green cards, but rather give the holder permission to work and reside in the United States for a specific time period, like current temporary worker visas.

Foreign workers on provisional visas will be allowed to switch jobs as long as they go to another employer with the required permit—that is, workers admitted under a particular type of provisional visa, such as a high-skilled visa, may move only to another employer who holds that type of permit. A foreign worker who loses a job and cannot find another must surrender his visa within a specified short period, perhaps a maximum of three months of unemployment, and depart the country. At any point in time, the number of provisional visa holders thus is equal to the number of permits plus a small number of unemployed visa holders who are searching for a new job.

Provisional visas will be renewable as long as the worker remains employed by an employer with a permit. The plan thus ends the notion of permanent residence as the primary means of immigration. A foreign worker will not necessarily be deciding to move permanently to the United States or "become an American," but rather will be choosing to work and reside in the country for a period of time. By not automatically issuing permanent residence to most new immigrants, the plan encourages return migration. Indeed, return migration of unemployed foreign workers—those who cannot find an employer with a permit willing to hire them—occurs automatically as long as there is work-site enforcement and no public assistance benefits for jobless workers.

The plan allows successful immigrants who remain employed and desire to stay to adjust to permanent resident status and, eventually, to become naturalized U.S. citizens. There will be no numerical limit on the number of people who can adjust their status, only on the number of new permits and hence new provisional work visa holders. This will end the current long queues of people waiting for green cards because of admissions category and country caps.

Foreign workers who wish to become permanent residents will face a waiting period. The waiting period should be shorter for high-skilled workers than for low-skilled workers because the former are larger contributors to the U.S. economy, and the country should encourage them to stay. High-skilled visa holders could be allowed to adjust to permanent resident status after working in the United States for five years, and low-skilled visa holders after ten years, for example. Other conditions, such as passing an English test, could also easily be applied at this stage to ensure integration into U.S. society.

Neither foreign workers holding a provisional visa nor any of their foreign-born dependents will be eligible for means-tested welfare benefits or social insurance programs. This includes unemployment insurance benefits, Medicaid, cash welfare, and the like. A very limited safety net will encourage foreign workers who lose their job to find another as quickly as possible or else leave the country. It will also minimize the adverse fiscal impacts of immigration.

Another way to limit the adverse fiscal impact of immigration, which, in the short run, is due in part to the cost of educating immigrants' children, is to require foreign workers who want to bring over dependents to pay a per-person fee. These fees will enable the federal government to assist states and localities in paying the additional education costs. There is ample precedent for charging for dependents to enter: the government already assesses a $300 fee per dependent entering on an H-4 visa and charges substantially higher per-person fees for most legal permanent resident applications. These funds also can be used to pay for programs that compensate natives displaced by foreign workers, such as job retraining programs.

Dependents will be limited to a spouse and minor unmarried children, who will be issued provisional nonwork visas. Spouses will be able to work as long as their employer holds the necessary permit; in that case, the spouse also receives a provisional work visa. These dependents may adjust to permanent resident status when the principal immigrant (the provisional work visa holder) does so.

A small, separate system involving self-sponsorship could be created for self-employed or entrepreneurial foreigners to ensure that the economy does not lose the benefits it reaps from such immigrants. There could be low- and high-skilled entrepreneurship permits where the entrepreneur would designate himself as the foreign hire. This system would function much like the current EB-5 investor program, which is premised on investing a certain amount of money or employing a certain number of workers. To allow for smaller-scale enterprises, it could also be based on having a certain dollar amount of sales. Immigrants who enter on a provisional work visa can convert over to a self-employment visa if they show a certain number of employees or amount in sales and eventually be eligible to adjust to permanent resident status.

An alternative way to foster entrepreneurship among immigrants who do not yet have permanent resident status is to allow workers to buy their permit from their employer and then be self-employed. For foreign workers who do not want to be self-employed but do want to switch employers, allowing permits to be resold directly to workers also might be an easy way to allow visa holders to move across firms. It might be easier for a new employer to reimburse a worker for the resale price of the permit rather than purchase a permit on the open market in order to hire that worker.

The Government's Role

Plan: The federal government periodically auctions permits to employers. An independent organization advises on the number of permits and the reserve prices. The federal government issues visas to foreign workers and accompanying dependents. It enforces all immigration laws and creates an accurate and timely employer verification system.

The federal government has several roles under the proposed plan. Its main new role is to determine the number of permits to sell in each category and time period and then to auction off those permits. An independent agency should be created to advise the federal government on how best to set the number of permits and the reserve price. The government will continue in its current law enforcement role; strict enforcement is necessary to discourage illegal immigration, and employer verification is necessary to ensure compliance with the plan. The government also will continue to screen new foreigners before issuing them visas.

The government needs to determine the initial quantity of permits available for auction and a target price range. The price range will act as a buffer, preventing the disruptive outcome of a very high or very low price. Another approach would be for the government to set a price and let the quantity fluctuate. Although this would allow the government to avoid making the highly politicized decision about how many permits there should be, it ignores the fact that establishing permit prices will initially be more difficult than determining permit quantities. There are years of data on migrant inflows to rely on for setting initial numerical targets, but there is no experience with firms bidding for the right to hire foreign workers to draw upon for setting prices. Moreover, the public might not tolerate large fluctuations in the numbers of permits as well as they would changes in permit prices.

Setting the quantity of permits will be both a practical and a strategic decision: practical in that a sudden drop in the number of new foreign workers could lead to large disruptions for employers who depend on such workers, and strategic in that the U.S. economy benefits more from certain types of immigrants than others. In the long run, the country benefits most from high-skilled workers, so immigration policy should increase the number of high-skilled worker permits faster than the number of permits for low-skilled and seasonal workers. The volume and composition of immigrant inflows in recent years provide a starting point for determining the optimal number of each type of permit to make available for auction.

As discussed in chapter 1, immigrants currently are admitted as legal permanent residents or as temporary workers on a variety of different visas. They also enter illegally. It is not a simple task to determine how many new immigrants work. Not only is it impossible to accurately estimate the inflow of undocumented workers, but information on the number of new legal immigrants who work is not publicly available.[10] Many legal permanent residents do not work, and some spouses of temporary visa holders can and do work legally. Average annual immigrant inflows and the approximate number of new workers during the period 2005–2008 were as follows:

- New legal permanent residents: 1.1 million per year. However, only 309,000 of those were adult new arrivals; the rest were adjusting from another status, such as temporary worker, or were minors. Among adult new arrivals, there were 21,000 employment-based immigrants (including spouses) per year; 29,000 diversity immigrants; and 256,000 family-sponsored immigrants. Estimates from the 2003 New Immigrant Survey suggest that about 75 percent of employment-based immigrants, 56 percent of diversity immigrants, and 47 percent of family-sponsored immigrants work.[11] This implies about 152,000 foreign-born legal permanent residents enter the labor market each year, assuming no change in labor force participation among immigrants adjusting status.

- Skilled temporary workers: 300,000 each year. This figure is based on issuances of H-1B and H-1B1 visas (high-skilled worker visas), H-1C visas (for nurses), L-1 intracompany transfer visas, TN visas and authorizations, O1 visas (for workers of extraordinary ability), and E1 and E2 (treaty traders and investors) visas.

- Low-skilled seasonal workers: 120,000 each year. The figure is based on issuances of H-2A and H-2B visas.

- Unauthorized immigrants: 500,000 each year. About 70 percent of these unauthorized immigrants, or 350,000 people, are in the labor force.[12]

The above estimates suggest that at least 920,000 immigrants enter the labor market each year. This number is an underestimate in that it does not count some categories of temporary worker visas or account for increases in labor force participation among immigrants adjusting to legal permanent resident status, such as a spouse who could not work while on an H-4 visa entering the labor market when she receives a green card. However, this undercount is offset by some return migration, particularly of temporary work visa holders and undocumented immigrants. These numbers provide a starting point for estimating the initial number of permits needed per year. The federal government can more accurately estimate the number of new foreign-born workers based on usage of newly issued Social Security numbers and other administrative data.

The next step is to figure out how many of each of the three permit types is needed. The skill composition of recent immigrant inflows suggests setting the initial annual number of permits in the following ranges:

- 345,000 to 395,000 high-skilled worker permits. This is approximately the number of high-skilled legal permanent residents who are new arrivals plus the number of high-skilled temporary worker visas issued annually.

- 225,000 to 275,000 low-skilled worker permits. This is approximately the number of low-skilled legal permanent residents who are new arrivals plus half of the average annual inflow of unauthorized workers in recent years.

- 275,000 to 325,000 seasonal worker permits. This is approximately the average number of H-2A and H-2B visas issued annually plus half of the average annual inflow of unauthorized workers.

This gives a total of 845,000 to 995,000 permits issued each year, with a midpoint of 920,000. This is the approximate number of immigrants entering the U.S. labor market annually in recent years, distributed across categories based on the current division. Some of these workers will continue to immigrate under the family provisions of our plan, so the lower end of our suggested range (about 850,000 permits) might be the most appropriate starting point. Again, policymakers should increase the emphasis on high-skilled workers by raising the number of those permits over time faster than the number of low-skilled and seasonal permits. In addition, the government might want to initially reduce the number of low-skilled and seasonal permits offered if a legalization plan is enacted alongside this worker-visa plan. Legalization would likely increase labor force participation by some current undocumented immigrants, particularly spouses, and decrease return migration, thus reducing the need in the short run to bring in low-skilled foreign workers.[13]

Along with setting the number of permits to be auctioned off in each category, the government should set a reserve price—a minimum price below which no permits are sold—for each type of permit. If no bids exceed the reserve price, no new permits are issued. In this way, the number of immigrants admitted becomes more responsive to market conditions; if demand is very low, no new foreign workers enter. For the initial auction, reserve prices could be set based on the cost of currently immigrating to the United States. Immigration lawyers charge $1,000 to $5,000 to process an H-1B application and the U.S. Citizenship and Immigration Service (USCIS) charges another $3,320.[14] After three years, the worker pays renewal fees under the current system. Hence, a reasonable initial reserve price for high-skilled worker permits that are valid for five years might be $10,000.

Low-skilled permits should have a lower reserve price to reflect the lower value added of those workers. A reasonable initial reserve price might be $6,000 for a five-year low-skilled permit. It currently costs about $2,000 to hire a coyote to smuggle an unauthorized immigrant across the U.S.-Mexico border.[15] A reasonable reserve price for seasonal permits therefore might be $2,000. For future auctions, the reserve price for each type could simply be the previous auction price for that type, adjusted for inflation. Alternatively, the reserve price could be adjusted to reflect the resale price of permits as well as changes in macroeconomic conditions.

The government might also consider setting a maximum price, which it would not disclose to bidders.[16] If bids exceed the maximum price, the government severely underestimated demand for foreign workers. It should then increase the number of permits available for sale at that auction. Adjusting the quantity of permits during the auction would reassure employers that future permit prices will not deviate too suddenly from past prices but rather that adjustments in permit prices will be gradual over short periods of time. Creating such a safety valve also forestalls disruptive changes in the resale market for permits.

Given the complexity and political sensitivity of running the permit auctions, the federal government should create an independent agency to give advice on or even set the number of permits and the reserve prices.[17] It is important to remove politics from the process to ensure that no special interests are favored. An independent agency or commission also probably would be able to make decisions in a timelier manner than Congress or the executive branch.

Making the number of new immigrants more responsive to the business cycle is one of the key advantages of the proposed plan. The government can reduce the number of new permits up for auction during a recession and can increase the number during an economic expansion. The government should adopt a transparent rule for setting the number of new permits available for sale in each category. This is where the resale market for permits becomes particularly useful—it provides information to the government about demand conditions for foreign workers. If permits are selling for more (less) than their initial price, it suggests that demand has risen (fallen) and the government should increase (decrease) the number of new permits it auctions off. The resale price needs to be adjusted for the fraction of time already used on that permit. For example, if only half the time on a five-year permit remains, its resale price should be multiplied by two to compare it with its initial price. The number of new permits could change proportionally with the difference between the resale price and the initial price.[18]

The proposed plan also generates government revenue, although some of this revenue simply replaces fees already in place. The plan's goal is not to maximize government revenue but rather to use prices as a tax, a signal of labor market tightness, and a selection device. The permit price is akin to a tax on foreign labor that varies with employer demand. The price mechanism makes foreign workers more expensive to hire than natives, so employers have an incentive to hire natives. The plan thus minimizes adverse effects on natives' labor market outcomes, one of the primary obstacles to immigration policy reform.

The permit price is also a signaling device. When employers' willingness to pay for foreign workers is low, the low price signals that fewer foreign workers should be admitted. Under the current system, in contrast, the same total number of legal permanent residents is admitted essentially regardless of employer demand.[19] If employers' demand for foreign workers is high, however, the price of those workers should rise, and that price increase provides a signal that the federal government should increase the number of permits auctioned during the next period.

Lastly, the permit price is a selection device that will help ensure an efficient allocation of foreign workers to U.S. employers. The current system relies on first-come, first-served or lotteries to hand out green cards and coveted temporary work visas. Under the auction system, foreign workers will be allocated to the employers who value them the most, which is where their expected productivity is the greatest.

Permit Auctions

Plan: Auctions are structured as a sealed-bid, single-price format, much like auctions for Treasury securities. The federal government creates or encourages a resale market in permits.

The federal government will hold auctions for new permits quarterly or semiannually. Frequent auctions are preferable, since they allow the number of permits and their prices to respond more quickly to economic conditions.

As permits expire, they will either be auctioned off again or "retired" from the market if demand is relatively low. The government can increase the number of permits simply by making more permits available for sale at a given reserve price (or by lowering the reserve price for a given number of permits if the reserve price is binding).

The auction's sealed-bid, single-price format works as follows. Employers submit bids indicating how many permits they would like to purchase and the price they are willing to pay. The bids are "sealed," or secret, to reduce possibilities for collusion. Permits are then allocated from highest to lowest price until the total number of permits is filled or the reserve price hit, whichever happens first. Winners pay the price of the lowest filled bid, so there is a uniform, or single, price for all permits of the same type sold at a given auction. Most permit holders thus end up paying less than their actual bid. This auction structure helps reduce concerns about the "winner's curse." The fact that most bidders will pay less than their bid makes them more willing to participate in the auction and to bid their true willingness to pay.[20] As we discuss below, moreover, the existence of a resale market also reduces bidders' risk, and should increase the number of participants and their willingness to pay.

Auctions should pose few problems for employers, particularly the large firms that currently sponsor most H-1B workers and employment-based legal permanent residents. The United States has well-established, successful auction markets for the wireless spectrum, offshore oil leases, and Treasury securities, among others, so many businesses are familiar with auctions. If there is concern that the auction format would unfairly privilege larger firms over smaller firms, a set proportion or number of permits could be held back for small firms (as measured by the number of employees or sales volume) and sold at the market-clearing price at the end of an auction.[21]

Having a resale market for permits is important. Employers will be more willing to purchase permits if they know they can resell the permits before expiration if no longer needed. The federal government could run an electronic resale market, where permit holders could specify prices at which they were willing to sell or potential buyers could indicate their prices at which they were willing to buy. Managing the resale market itself (as opposed to having an independent market) makes it easier for the federal government to keep track of who holds permits and what the resale prices are. As noted above, the resale market provides valuable information to the government or an independent agency for use in designing future auctions.

Several economists have suggested that the government auction off visas. Gary Becker, Barry Chiswick, Richard Freeman, Gordon Hanson and Julian Simon are among those who have recommended that the government auction off the right to immigrate to the United States.[22] Some of these economists suggested auctioning visas directly to immigrants themselves rather than auctioning permits to hire foreign workers to employers. The appeal of auctioning off visas directly to would-be immigrants is twofold: maximize revenue by auctioning visas to those who value them most, the immigrants themselves; and permit immigrants to choose where or whether to work within the United States after they acquire a visa.

The plan developed here instead focuses on auctions to employers. The benefit of our plan is that employment-based immigration selects the most productive foreign workers, which in turn is most likely to boost economic growth and efficiency. Moreover, auctioning visas directly to immigrants may be untenable. Many potential immigrants face credit constraints and would not be able to borrow the funds to pay for a visa in an auction. Of course, the government or the private sector could set up programs to lend funds to potential immigrants, but the administrative costs and default rates might be high.

Family-Based Immigration

> **Plan: U.S. citizens may sponsor a spouse and minor unmarried children for legal permanent residence. They may no longer sponsor parents, siblings, or other children. Permanent residents and provisional visa holders must pay a fee to bring over dependents. Permanent residents may no longer sponsor adult children.**

Immediate relatives of U.S. citizens will continue to be allowed in without limit and granted permanent resident status. However, immediate relatives will be defined as spouses and unmarried minor children and will no longer include parents, older children, or married children.[23] Spouses and minor unmarried children of U.S. citizens accounted for over one-third of new green card recipients during fiscal years 2004 to 2008.[24] This is clearly an important, indeed sacrosanct, category and should continue to be unlimited (although subject to scrutiny to make sure marriages are valid).

Our plan eliminates the current family-sponsored structure that allows adult or married children of U.S. citizens or permanent residents and parents and siblings of U.S. citizens (and their spouses and children) to receive permanent resident status. Such family reunification immigrants comprised almost 20 percent of all people granted permanent resident status in fiscal years 2005 to 2008.[25] Eliminating these categories is necessary to prioritize employment-based immigration, limit the fiscal burden of family-based migration, and slow chain migration. U.S. immigration policy has been exceedingly generous with regard to family migration over the last few decades. And while it is honorable and generous to reunite U.S. citizens with their foreign-born siblings and elderly parents, it is costly and does not necessarily serve the broader national interest. Compared with other immigrant groups, these immigrants tend to have low education levels, employment rates, and earnings as well as poor English-language fluency; they vie with refugees and asylees for the bottom of the skill distribution among green card recipients.[26]

Decreasing the number of visas available for relatives may seem counter to the humanitarian and inclusive nature of U.S. immigration policy. But such values should not necessarily trump economic considerations to the extent they do under current policy, which heavily favors relatives. Families should remember that migrating to the United States was, for most, a voluntary choice; being able to sponsor one's relatives is not a right that need automatically accompany a green card or naturalized U.S. citizenship. Humanitarian considerations in favor of family reunification were more compelling in the Cold War era when they were implemented. At that time, many families separated by migration would never see each other again. Nowadays, separation does not impose the same hardships it once did. The collapse of the Iron Curtain and falling costs of travel and telecommunications help family members remain connected even if they live in different countries.

The plan developed here charges a fee to permanent residents and provisional work visa holders who bring over a spouse or minor children. This fee helps offset some of the costs that such dependents impose, on average. Dependents who are present in the United States when the principal worker adjusts status will also receive permanent resident status. However, dependents of permanent residents who arrive after the principal adjusts status will receive provisional nonwork visas; they will be able to adjust to permanent resident status after a five-year period. This plan thus eliminates the queue of spouses and minor children of permanent residents waiting to enter, a queue that has a current wait time of some five years. The tradeoff is that those migrants do not immediately receive a green card and are not immediately eligible to work (unless hired by an employer with a permit, of course).

Dependents of provisional visa holders would also get provisional nonwork visas, with the length of stay tied to the principal's work visa. The fee for bringing over family members could be lower for holders of high-skilled provisional visas, since their dependents will likely contribute more to the U.S. economy if they remain in the United States permanently, although such a provision might be politically contentious. In order to encourage return migration of seasonal workers, the federal government might bar holders of seasonal work visas from bringing over dependents, as is the case with H-2B visas under current law.

The Current Queue

Plan: The current green card queue is cleared by granting provisional visas to those already in the United States and exempting them from the employer permit requirement. Those not yet in the United States who are not an immediate relative of a U.S. citizen or permanent resident under the new definition are removed from the queue and refunded their application fees.

An important question that any substantial immigration policy reform needs to address is what to do about foreigners in the green card queue when the laws are changed. Under current policy, applicants in oversubscribed categories are put on a waiting list after their permanent resident petition is approved. Some are waiting because of preference category caps, some because of country-of-origin caps, and some because of both. Some will wait for well over a decade before they can get legal permanent residence in the United States. Possible ways to deal with these potential immigrants include grandfathering them in and allowing them to continue to enter as scheduled while reducing the number of visas available for auction proportionally; somehow giving them preference under the new system; or voiding the queue and starting from scratch.

Our plan would clear the current queue by giving those already residing in the United States provisional work visas or provisional nonwork visas. In the case of workers, these visas would be exempt from the employer permit requirement, but fees would still have to be paid for dependents. Not applying the permit requirement to these provisional immigrants gives them a leg up in keeping their current job or getting a new job, but the plan still ties their entry to work more closely than does the current system. These provisional immigrants would be eligible to adjust to permanent resident status after five years, provided they remain employed if on a provisional work visa. Dependents who want to work would be allowed to convert to provisional work visas that also are exempt from the employer permit requirement.[27] Unlike the provisional work visas our proposal calls for, which require that the employer have a permit, these work visas will not distinguish between high- and low-skilled workers.

Most immigrants currently in the queue for employer-sponsored visas should be able to receive a provisional work visa under the proposed scheme. As of 2006, over one million people were waiting for employer-sponsored green cards.[28] Much of this backlog is due to country caps, which the reforms proposed here discard. Many of these people are already working and living in the United States, so they would simply convert from a temporary worker visa to a provisional work visa. Such current temporary work visa holders could be given credit for years already worked under the current visa toward the five- or ten-year period required before adjusting to permanent resident status. The remainder of the current queue for employer-sponsored green cards—people not already working in the United States—is likely to receive provisional work visas; these people will enter the country when their sponsoring employers purchase permits.

Over 2.7 million people are currently waiting for family-sponsored green cards. This queue consists of three groups: people already living in the United States;[29] people living abroad who are spouses or minor unmarried children of legal permanent residents; and people living abroad who are other relatives of U.S. citizens or legal permanent residents. Those who are already living in the United States will receive provisional visas, as will people living abroad who are spouses or minor unmarried children of legal permanent residents. People not already in the United States who are not an immediate relative of a U.S. citizen or permanent resident under the new definition will be refunded their application fees. Although they will be taken out of the queue, many of them may be able to enter the United States—perhaps more quickly than under the current regime—since the plan proposed here includes a substantial number of visas for low-skilled workers. Because they have relatives already in the United States, people currently in the queue for family-sponsored visas may be able to utilize immigrant networks and find an employer willing to bring them in on a low-skilled worker visa.

Illegal Immigration

Plan: Employers are required to verify that workers are here legally or face penalties for noncompliance. Current illegal immigrant workers and their dependents are eligible for a variant of the new provisional visa. Unauthorized immigrants who came as children and have earned a U.S. high school diploma or GED are immediately eligible for provisional permanent resident status.

Comprehensive reform needs not only to plan for future immigrant inflows but also to drastically reduce the incentive for future illegal immigration and deal with the unauthorized immigrants currently present in the country. The plan proposed here depends crucially on strict enforcement of immigration and labor laws. Because the plan essentially taxes employers who hire foreign labor by requiring that they buy a permit, the presence of unauthorized immigrants would undermine the plan—undocumented immigrants would continue to be a cheaper source of labor than natives or legal foreign workers. The government therefore must be able to require verification of virtually all workers' legal status in an easy, fast, low-cost, and foolproof manner. Any employer who withholds taxes for an employee—foreign or native—should be required to verify the worker's eligibility to work legally.[30] Setting up an accurate electronic database and enforcing sizable penalties for employers who hire unauthorized immigrants are vital to the success of the plan.

Accurate verification likely will require a biometric identification card. We acknowledge the concerns about privacy raised by the use of such cards; certainly any system must be carefully designed with safeguards. This book focuses on the economics of immigration policy reform, however, and we leave such issues to law enforcement experts. We do note that an accurate verification system actually can help ethnic minorities who are legally present in the United States. Research suggests that Hispanics faced labor market discrimination in the immediate post-IRCA period, that is, before employers realized that the law had no teeth regarding penalties for hiring unauthorized immigrants. Wages and employment declined among Hispanics who were legally present, including some born in the United States, because employers had difficulty distinguishing between legal and unauthorized workers.[31] A good verification system should prevent such adverse effects from occurring among minorities as a by-product of stepped-up employer enforcement.

Of course, it is wishful thinking to believe that the United States can curtail illegal immigration completely. Some unauthorized immigrants will enter and work no matter how many obstacles the government creates. Further, eliminating all illegal immigration would be inefficient. From a purely economic perspective, the United States should spend resources to reduce illegal immigration as long as the gains from doing so exceed the costs.[32] Current enforcement measures, particularly interior work-site enforcement, fall well below this threshold and clearly should be increased. Other measures, such as border patrol, already may have passed beyond this point. It is critical that immigration policy seek to eliminate the main incentive for people to enter illegally—employment—by making it expensive and inefficient for employers to hire unauthorized workers. This is best done through a combination of carrots, or a way for employers to bring in low-skilled workers legally, and sticks, or penalties for hiring undocumented workers.

The government must decide whether to legalize or deport unauthorized immigrants who are already in the United States. Decades of lax enforcement in the face of mass illegal immigration are impossible to reverse at this point without incurring huge costs, both monetary and humanitarian. Mass deportation of eleven million undocumented immigrants is not practical or humane. Immigration reform therefore should include a legalization program for qualified unauthorized immigrants already present in the country. Adult unauthorized immigrants who have committed no other serious crimes will be required to present documentation of their U.S. residence and to pay back taxes and a large fine. In exchange, they will be given a five-year renewable work visa, which will be exempt from the employer permit requirement so that these workers can remain in their current jobs.

These workers will be eligible to apply for permanent resident status after ten years and U.S. citizenship after an additional five years. They will wait longer to be eligible for permanent residence than people already in the green card queue, who also receive provisional visas but who must wait only five years to adjust status and do not have to pay any fees. This penalizes those who broke the law but not those who played by the rules.

Nonworking dependents who also are illegal aliens could remain legally on provisional nonwork visas as long as they pass similar background checks and pay sizable fines and the dependent visa fees. They eventually would be eligible for permanent resident status as dependents of the principal applicant. To encourage labor force participation, these dependents would be allowed to convert to provisional work visas that are exempt from the employer permit requirement. In either case, they would face the ten-year timelines to legal permanent resident status and naturalization after adjusting to provisional status.

There should be one exception to this plan: unauthorized immigrants who came as children and have earned a high school diploma or GED in the United States. A separate plan should be created for this group because they did not choose to illegally enter the country. They have demonstrated a minimum skill level by earning a high school diploma or GED, they speak English well, and they are therefore qualified for better jobs than low-skilled provisional work visa holders are likely to hold. Conditional on not having a criminal record, these unauthorized immigrants should be given provisional permanent resident status and be allowed to work for any employer, not just one with a permit. Any fines or fees should be lower for this group than for other unauthorized immigrants because they did not choose to break the law—their parents made that choice for them—and they have completed a high school education. Incorporating these young adults into the legitimate labor force and encouraging them to work and acquire more human capital is in the country's best interest. They should receive a green card after a specified period, perhaps two years, of working, being enrolled in college, or serving in the military.

The Benefits of Legalization Outweigh the Costs. There are many benefits to legalization if done properly. Undocumented immigrant workers who were formerly paid "off the books" will come into compliance with tax laws. Tax receipts will increase.[33] These workers' wages and benefits will likely rise, and the share without health insurance will fall.[34] Newly legalized immigrants will be better able to access banking services, credit, and loans. They will increase their training and schooling, be more likely to start businesses, learn English faster, and assimilate sooner. Their children will have better outcomes. Former illegal immigrants will no longer fear contacting police or other emergency services if they become victims of crime, witness a crime, or need medical attention.

There are also costs of legalization, although most of these can be avoided or mitigated with a well-crafted plan. One potential cost of legalization is a higher rate of welfare recipiency and hence higher program costs as former undocumented immigrants get access to public assistance programs. However, this problem can be addressed by limiting legalized immigrants' eligibility for public assistance programs for a set number of years. Another potential difficulty is that newly legalized immigrants will likely want to sponsor relatives for immigration as soon as they are able, which would lead to explosive chain migration much like the United States has experienced in the wake of the 1986 IRCA legalization. This will not occur under the plan outlined here, because it cuts off family-based immigration except for spouses and unmarried minor children.

Additional costs of legalization on which critics focus heavily are the perception that an amnesty rewards lawbreakers and will encourage more people to enter and work illegally in hopes of another legalization program. It is true that legalization entails forgiving offenders for the misdemeanor crime of illegal entry or visa overstay. Our plan includes a hefty fine to penalize unauthorized immigrants for their transgressions. On the other hand, it releases employers who hired undocumented workers in the past from any civil or criminal liability. Penalizing employers would give them an incentive to fire unauthorized workers or to deny them the paperwork needed to prove they have been employed and have had taxes withheld. It might also lead to long and expensive legal battles for the government, which would have to show that employers had knowingly hired unauthorized immigrants.

Will a legalization program lead to continued illegal entry and work by people hoping for another amnesty program in the future? After all, one of the main goals of immigration reform is to minimize unauthorized immigration. The lessons from IRCA are not particularly promising here. Apprehensions along the U.S.-Mexico border slowed in the immediate post-IRCA period but then resumed their prelegalization trend, suggesting that IRCA failed to stop undocumented immigration. There are several reasons for this: IRCA did not create a viable way for large numbers of nonseasonal low-skilled workers to enter legally, the law's provisions for verifying legal status were easily skirted, and few employers were punished for hiring unauthorized workers. Under the "wink and a nod" system, there was no obstacle to employment as long as workers could provide something that resembled the correct forms of identification.

The plan proposed here avoids the mistakes of IRCA. It includes an accurate, fast, easy verification system accompanied by penalties for employers who do not use it. Cutting off employment prospects is the surest way to stem illegal immigration. In addition, employers are unlikely to revert to hiring unauthorized immigrants if, as part of comprehensive reform, there is a way for them to bring in sufficient numbers of workers legally on either low-skilled or seasonal worker visas.

There should be penalties for breaking the law, but some aspects of previous legalization proposals went too far. In the 2006 and 2007 immigration reform bills discussed in chapter 2, for example, legalization beneficiaries had to pay back taxes and a fine along with fulfilling various other requirements, but be last in line for green cards, i.e., wait until the entire queue at the time of the bill's passage had been cleared.[35] The bills also had a "touch back" provision of some sort where certain unauthorized immigrants had to return to their home country temporarily, while more recent arrivals had to depart permanently. While some of these measures make sense from an economic perspective, others have little benefit relative to the cost. Why make immigrants spend the money to return home and then reenter instead of just raising the legalization fee and thereby capturing those funds for the Treasury? Why favor people who are lucky enough to have a relative already in the United States willing to sponsor them for permanent resident status over people who have been working here and paying taxes for years? Better to enact a legalization process that quickly converts illegal immigrants into legal workers who pay full taxes and have incentives to integrate.

High-Immigrant Communities

Plan: States and localities with large numbers of immigrants receive a share of funds from permit auctions in order to offset any adverse fiscal impact they experience.

Part of the opposition to continued high levels of immigration is centered on concerns that immigrants are a fiscal burden, imposing greater costs on public coffers than they pay in taxes. As discussed earlier, this claim is indeed true for immigrants who do not have a high school diploma or equivalent; on average, more-educated immigrants pay more in taxes than they use in services. Completely curtailing low-skilled immigration is not the answer, however. The economy needs such workers. Instead, the government should reallocate some of the gains from immigration to the communities that are most affected by low-skilled immigration.

The adverse fiscal impact of immigration is concentrated in particular areas within the United States. Almost one-half of the foreign-born population (compared with less than one-fourth of natives) lives in just three states: California, New York, and Texas.[36] Low-education immigrants are even more concentrated: 55 percent of adult immigrants who do not have a high school diploma live in those three states, versus 20 percent of comparable natives. Although the foreign-born population began to disperse more widely during the 1990s, moving into the Southeast and Mountain States in unprecedented numbers, they nonetheless remain much more geographically concentrated than natives.

This geographic concentration means that certain areas disproportionately bear the costs associated with low-skilled immigration. Only half of immigrants have private health insurance, compared with 70 percent of natives.[37] Households headed by an immigrant have more children than households headed by a native. On average, for every ten households, those headed by immigrants have four more children than those headed by natives.[38] These differences mean that state and local governments in areas with large numbers of low-wage immigrants are faced with higher health care and educational costs. The National Research Council estimated that in 1996, the average immigrant-headed household in New Jersey received $1,484 more in state and local services than it paid in taxes, while the average immigrant-headed household in California received a net transfer of $3,463.[39]

The plan proposed here creates a simple way to compensate areas that are struggling with providing services for immigrants, and hence to reduce opposition to immigration reform: transfer some of the funds from the permit auctions to those areas. The federal government could redistribute a share of those funds to state and local governments and school districts based on the geographic distribution of provisional visa holders. Since low-skilled immigrants tend to impose greater costs, the redistribution scheme could allocate more funds to areas with large proportions of low-skilled and seasonal visa holders than to areas with large proportions of high-skilled visa holders. The fees charged for accompanying dependent children could go directly to states and localities to offset educational costs. Such redistribution would also help reduce opposition to immigration reform.

Conclusion

The immigration policy outlined in detail above replaces the current inefficient and outdated system with a simple and efficient tax scheme where employers bid for permits to hire foreign workers. The government holds permit auctions, and the permit prices create both a disincentive for employers to use foreign labor and a source of revenue for U.S. taxpayers. Permits in hand, employers can hire foreign workers, who are then issued provisional visas. Family-based migration is limited under this plan; this approach prioritizes visas for the workers employers want to hire and reduces the chain migration that can lead to adverse fiscal impacts on destination communities. The bulk of immigrants will come in under provisional visas, not green cards, although adjustment to permanent resident status is possible over time if certain conditions are met.

Our policy removes many poorly designed aspects of the current immigration system. By channeling more visas to high-skilled workers, it is more selective. It is also more efficient because it eliminates queuing, preference categories, and country quotas. Our proposed policy is also more flexible and responsive to market conditions. An advisory commission will help decide how many permits to auction off, based on real-time data on economic growth and labor market tightness. The volume of recent immigrant inflows suggests auctioning off about 850,000 permits, with 25 to 30 percent going to low-skilled workers, 25 to 30 percent to seasonal workers, and up to 40 percent to high-skilled workers. Over time, the high-skilled proportion could be gradually increased.

The proposal here includes provisional visas for most unauthorized immigrants. They would need to pay appropriate fines and fees and meet additional requirements in order to earn permanent resident status, and the wait would be at least ten years. Unauthorized immigrants who came as children and have completed high school would be fast-tracked to green cards. Immigrants who are currently in the green card queue and living and working in the United States would receive provisional visas and be eligible for permanent resident status over time.

The plan consists of policies intended not only to speed up and simplify the immigration process but also to win the support of different constituents. It does not build upon the current confused system but starts fresh, which requires some practical solutions to thorny problems, such as legalizing the undocumented population and clearing the current green card queues. Some compromises must be made along the route to a better immigration policy, and the compromises suggested here aim to limit costs while also trying to be as fair as practicable.

4

What the Plan Does Not Include
and Why

Our plan is for comprehensive immigration reform aimed at engendering efficiency and flexibility in the nation's immigration policy and enhancing the credibility of the government that is charged with enforcing the new laws. The main objectives are to enhance economic growth, mitigate negative labor-market effects, reduce adverse fiscal impacts, and limit illegal immigration. These goals are met by basing immigration primarily on employment rather than family ties, and specifically by auctioning permits to employers who want to hire high- and low-skilled foreign workers. The plan also calls for legalization of most unauthorized immigrants.

For readers who remain unconvinced and are still searching for options, this chapter addresses alternative immigration reforms, ranging from what is practiced in other countries, such as a point system or a guest-worker program, to more extreme options like completely open immigration, mass deportation, or an end to birthright citizenship. We stress that our proposal is likely a better option than any of these, particularly when considering the goals laid out in chapter 2.

Why Not Use a Point System?

Australia, Canada, New Zealand, and, most recently, the United Kingdom are among the countries that use point systems to encourage high-skilled immigration. These countries allocate points based on education, language proficiency (English and French for Canada, just English for the others), years of work experience in a high-skilled occupation, and low age. Points are also awarded for having a job offer already in hand, having work experience and education in that country, having a more skilled partner/spouse, and having family already living in the country. The point system's emphasis is on skills—family ties alone are nowhere near sufficient to meet the threshold required to immigrate in countries that use these systems.

Advocates of a point system for the United States frequently note that Australia and Canada attract more skilled immigrants than the United States and claim that more U.S. immigrants would be highly skilled if the United States relied on a point system.[1] It is true that immigrant-native earnings gaps are considerably smaller in those countries than in the United States, and immigrants' education levels tend to be higher.[2] However, researchers note that this cross-country difference may be due more to geography than to immigration policy—unlike Canada and Australia, the United States has a long border with a developing country (Mexico) that is its primary source of low-skilled immigrants. Geography appears to matter at least as much as immigration policy for the skill level of incoming migrants.[3] Adopting a point system that excludes low-skilled workers from Mexico would simply lead to continued unauthorized immigration to the United States absent extremely strict and costly border and interior enforcement.

There are several additional limitations to a point system. First, immigrants can enter without having employment if they have enough points in other categories. As a result, immigrants who come in under point systems have higher unemployment rates than those who come in under employment-based systems.[4] Second, a simple point system that essentially excludes low-skilled workers fails to address the desires of many employers and consumers. A point system can be used to give preference to skilled workers or to unskilled workers but not both. Third, most point systems are rigid— the number of immigrants admitted typically does not vary with the host country's business cycle absent government-initiated changes, such as an increase in the threshold. Responding to changes in the demand for foreign workers thus requires changing the point system, a lengthy process if the U.S. Congress needs to be involved (although more nimble in countries with parliamentary systems of government). An auction system, in contrast, responds quickly to changes in economic conditions.

Another concern about a point system is how the government will determine what certain characteristics are worth. Should older immigrants be penalized? How many points should be awarded on the basis of family ties? But an even greater concern about a point system is whether it guarantees that employers can get foreign workers with desired skills. Allocating points correctly requires an immense amount of knowledge—and some arbitrary judgment calls—by Congress or whatever body sets the points. Employment-based immigration in combination with a permit auction is better because auctions use a price system to effectively determine how to best allocate points. Employers who benefit the most from foreign workers presumably bid the most, and visas are allocated to their highest valued use without government intervention. Allowing markets to work instead of relying on government bureaucrats, who would need to know employers' relative demand for every possible type of worker, is a key reason why an auction system is better than a point system. An auction system also raises revenue in the process.

Further, immigrant assimilation in countries with point systems is far from perfect. Even though immigrants in those countries are more skilled than in the United States, they still face problems with skill transferability and discrimination.[5] Indeed, the unemployment rate among new immigrants is higher in Australia than in the United States.[6] Immigrants entering Canada under skilled admission classes during the early 2000s were actually more likely to be poor, both at entry and chronically, than immigrants admitted under family reunification provisions.[7] A point system alone is not sufficient: it needs to be combined with programs aimed at encouraging immigrant integration as well as policies that deter undocumented immigration.

Despite these concerns, a well-designed point system that puts considerable weight on having a job offer would certainly be a vast improvement over current U.S. policy. If the United States adopts a point system, it should admit most immigrants on a provisional basis instead of automatically granting permanent residence upon entry. Immigrants should be allowed to remain and adjust to permanent resident status if they meet work and other requirements, such as learning English. A point system also needs to be designed with enough flexibility to quickly adapt to changes in labor demand. Instead of relying on Congress to determine how points are awarded, a commission of experts should be created with the authority to respond regularly to changes in employers' demand for foreign workers.

Why Not Allow Open Immigration?

A radical immigration reform would be to provide an unlimited number of visas, allowing anyone who can pass a background check and wants to enter to immigrate. This certainly has the virtue of simplicity. In addition, strong moral arguments can be made for not restricting immigration at all. Such arguments can take several forms.[8] One could argue that the United States has a moral obligation to reduce the enormous global disparities in living standards and that ending restrictions on international migration is a necessary, indeed perhaps the best, means to reduce such disparities. One could also argue that migration is a human right, which nations are obliged to protect. One could take the cosmopolitan view that national borders are artificial constructs and all human beings belong to a single community. There is then no reason to favor the interests of U.S. natives over those of the rest of the world, and all barriers to trade and migration should be removed.

We leave such moral arguments to the philosophers and adopt a more practical stance here. There are several reasons why open immigration is unrealistic: immigration would significantly increase, home-country conditions would drive migration, fiscal costs would increase for U.S. taxpayers, U.S. wages would likely fall, and immigrant assimilation would slow. The potential adverse effects on source countries offer additional reasons not to allow open immigration.

Under open immigration, immigrant inflows would increase as barriers to entry, such as a job or family ties, are removed. Home-country conditions would drive migration, and gains to the United States would likely be smaller than when U.S. economic forces motivate migration. One of the main benefits of migration is its timely delivery of a needed labor supply: when the U.S. economy grows and wages rise, immigration increases, and when the economy contracts, immigration slows. Immigration controls must be maintained in order for this vital correlation to persist. Under open immigration, home-country conditions could come to drive migration flows to the host country. Hurricanes in Honduras, war in Iraq, political oppression in China, economic crisis in Mexico—any number of global catastrophes would cause U.S. migration to surge regardless of the ability of the nation to absorb the influx. Some humanitarian migration is essential, but the ability to serve immigrants is reduced when the volume suddenly rises.

Milton Friedman noted frequently that open immigration is fundamentally incompatible with the existence of the welfare state.[9] Under current policy, immigrants are fully eligible for welfare benefits after they naturalize, and their U.S.-born children are eligible on the same terms as all other U.S. citizens. Even the most extreme policy—one that bars all foreign born from public assistance for their lifetimes—would still face enormous costs associated with providing health care and education for immigrants' children under an open immigration regime. Setting up a two-tiered system that treats some citizens differently from others would violate the same principles that justify open immigration.

U.S. wages would likely fall under open immigration. Completely unrestricted immigration would essentially speed up what economists call "factor price equalization"—wages in the United States would converge to levels found in other countries, adjusted for differences in productivity and purchasing power. Of course, wages in the United States would still be higher than in developing countries because of higher levels of physical and human capital here, but the differences would be smaller than now. The immigration surplus under open immigration would be large, but the distribution of gains would be problematic. Owners of capital and the migrants themselves would benefit, while competing workers would see reduced wages or employment losses. Congestion would drive up transportation and housing costs, at least in the short to medium run. For open immigration not to lead to economic dislocations, it would need to be combined with a large redistribution plan to reallocate some of those gains to workers who would suffer losses. Such redistribution seems antithetical to the libertarian flavor of a call for open immigration.

Immigrant integration would slow under an open policy, as large numbers of immigrants would likely form ethnic neighborhoods where they would come into little contact with English, U.S. natives, and U.S. culture. Although living among compatriots can help immigrants find jobs when they first arrive, it harms labor market outcomes over the long run. Its effects on the second generation can be particularly pernicious.

Unrestricted immigration would have a major economic impact not only in the United States but also in source countries. On the positive side, high emigration rates in developing countries would raise wages there and boost remittances to relatives left behind.[10] However, the people most likely to leave are unlikely to be the very poorest of the poor, who cannot afford to migrate. Some countries would risk losing a high enough share of their young adult labor force or of their high-skilled workers as to slow economic growth. It is hard to predict the exact consequences of open immigration for source countries, and the effects would likely change over time, but there are certainly downside risks.

A variation on open immigration that may be more reasonable is to allow unrestricted labor migration within the NAFTA zone.[11] After all, why allow free trade in goods but not in labor? We already have what is essentially free movement of high-skilled workers from Canada and Mexico into the United States through the TN visa. A NAFTA common labor market could be modeled on the EU system, with a gradual opening up of borders to allow for easier adjustment. A common labor market would likely increase out-migration of low-skilled workers from Mexico to the United States and Canada. Some relatively small-scale movement of more-skilled workers across the three countries would probably occur as well.[12]

Nevertheless, the economic implications of a NAFTA common labor market are nontrivial. Because of the disparity in skill distributions between the United States and Canada vis-à-vis Mexico, a common labor market would likely cause wages to fall at the bottom of the distribution in the first two countries while raising them in the third. Low-skilled U.S. workers have already been experiencing declining real wages for decades. This additional drop in their incomes would almost surely make such a plan politically infeasible. Another complication is whether and how to harmonize taxes and pensions and set welfare benefits so as to limit any adverse fiscal impact on the United States and Canada.

On the other hand, mass out-migration from Mexico may prove short-lived. Changes in Mexico's demographics suggest labor surpluses will not endure for much longer.[13] Mexico is currently undergoing what is one of the biggest demographic transitions in world history. Births per Mexican woman have declined from above six in 1970 to below three in 2008.[14] Immigrant inflows from Mexico thus will be much smaller within two generations, and living standards there should be considerably higher, even absent the safety valve that immigration to the United States provides.

Finally, a NAFTA labor market would not provide enough high-skilled immigrants. EU member countries have reached similar conclusions about their system: integration within Europe is not enough, and programs that reach outside Europe and bring in talent (similar to the U.S. H-1B program) are needed. Despite immigration by high-skilled Canadians and Mexicans, the United States would still need to combine a NAFTA labor market with another mechanism for attracting high-skilled workers. Open immigration, even if just within North America, is not a solution to the United States' immigration conundrum.

Why Not Have a Guest-Worker Program?

Creating a guest-worker program is a frequently mentioned immigration reform. There are several potential benefits from such a program. A guest-worker program that brings in low-skilled workers temporarily to do essential but low-paying jobs could create a legal means of entry for workers who would otherwise enter illegally. It could reduce exploitation of such workers and make it easier for the federal government to enforce employment regulations relative to the current situation where hundreds of thousands of unauthorized workers enter the country each year, many to live and work in the shadows. It also could reduce adverse fiscal impacts of immigration by imposing a tax or fee on the workers or their employers; it could also stipulate that guest workers not be eligible for any social assistance benefits and that they not bring in dependents. It is relatively easy to change the number of guest-worker visas issued in response to the business cycle. For all of these reasons, a guest-worker program has much to commend it.

However, a guest-worker program has two key downsides. First, how does the government make sure the guest workers go home? Germany created a large-scale guest-worker program in the 1960s intended to bring in temporary workers. Many of these workers stayed and brought over spouses, leading to a permanent, poorly integrated immigrant population.[15] The U.S. experience with the *braceros* also suggests that it is difficult to ensure that temporary migrants return home; when that program ended, many of those workers continued to enter but as unauthorized immigrants.

Of course, there are mechanisms that can be adopted to encourage guest workers to leave. Carrots include paying bonuses to guest workers who return home, and creating a pension system for returning guest workers in the home country. Sticks include requiring guest workers or their employer to post a bond that is returned when the worker leaves (or adjusts to permanent resident status) but is forfeited if the worker does not leave, and deporting guest workers who do not leave voluntarily. Regardless, many guest workers may be reluctant to leave, particularly those who marry and have children in the United States.

The second problem with guest-worker programs is that guest workers tend to get exploited. The *bracero* program was ended following public outrage over the working conditions of farm workers. Guest workers tend to be vulnerable to exploitation because they are tied to a single employer, or the middleman involved in matching them with an employer may be dishonest. Moreover, home governments who administer guest-worker programs may themselves be corrupt; millions of dollars of the *braceros'* repatriated earnings were somehow "lost" as they were sent back to Mexico in the 1950s and 1960s.[16] A well-crafted guest-worker program therefore faces the difficult challenge of being easy to use and administer yet fair and safe for workers.

The plan outlined in chapter 3 tries to capture the benefits of a guest-worker program but avoid the pitfalls. The plan resembles a guest-worker program in that it admits workers provisionally for an initial specified period. The aim is to facilitate good matches between employers and employees and to reduce harms to competing workers and taxpayers. Unlike a guest-worker program, however, the plan proposed here allows those workers to move across employers and creates a clear path to permanent residence for successful immigrants. It acknowledges that many foreign workers will want to remain and that the United States benefits when economically successful immigrants stay.

If immigration reform includes a guest-worker program, it should allow workers to switch employers and should limit the role of middlemen and foreign governments, who often exploit workers and extract some of their hard-earned gains. It should include a provision for some workers to remain and also a mechanism to ensure that workers without jobs return. It should vary the number of guest workers with the business cycle. And it should use a mechanism (such as auctions) for allocating guest-worker visas on a more efficient basis than simply first come, first served. If other visa programs remain in place, the United States would need to accommodate about 300,000 to 400,000 guest workers in a typical year.

Should a guest-worker program be focused on a specific country or region? Since most low-skilled migrants come from Mexico and Central America, it would probably make sense to have a special program for nationals of those countries. However, since most low-skilled migrants come from those countries without a visa, it likely means a special visa does not have to be devised for them. They will be the natural hires for low-skilled positions since they are geographically close and already have extensive U.S. networks. Moreover, the thrust of immigration reform is to design a policy that will stand the test of time. Mexico is on the cusp of a major demographic transition. With the dramatic drop in births in recent decades, demographers suggest there will be a decline in future migration from Mexico. So while a guest-worker or special visa program with Mexico might not be an ill-advised policy, particularly in the short run, such a narrow focus would limit the scope and flexibility of the new immigration system.

Why Not Deport All Unauthorized Immigrants?

Some critics of the current immigration system argue that the United States should engage in mass deportations of unauthorized immigrants.[17] They argue that these people have no legal right to be in the country and therefore should be given a choice to leave voluntarily or be forcibly removed. Deportation proponents argue that mass deportations would enhance national security, reduce crime, raise the wages and employment prospects of competing workers, and reduce the fiscal burden associated with immigration.

The previous chapter touched briefly on why the United States should not deport all unauthorized immigrants. We elaborate the reasons here. First, deportation is inhumane. Unauthorized immigrants have lived and worked in the United States for years. They have put down roots and created families. Their children are typically U.S. citizens. Second, mass deportation is completely impractical because of the costs. The direct costs of deportation are estimated to exceed $200 billion over a five-year period.[18] The indirect costs include the severe economic disruption that would ensue as the labor of eight million undocumented immigrant workers is taken out of the economy and as these individuals default on mortgages, car loans, and credit cards. There would also be indirect costs in the form of a paralyzed legal system, with courts flooded by immigrants' petitions to remain. There would be higher prices for goods and services that those workers—who make up about 5 percent of the labor force—supplied.

Third, deportation is a temporary and ineffective solution to a long-standing problem. Deporting undocumented workers has the paradoxical effect of raising wages in sectors that employ such workers, which in turn increases the incentives for more illegal immigration. An expensive cat-and-mouse game can quickly develop if no legal channel is created through which low-skilled workers can enter.

Additionally, deporting undocumented immigrants would not do much to punish the employers who hire them or to discourage them from hiring more unauthorized workers. Employers of undocumented immigrants would face higher labor costs as a result of deportations, but would likely hire unauthorized immigrants again if they do not face fines or other sanctions. Despite some well-publicized workplace raids, the federal government emphasizes border enforcement over work-site enforcement, and even the latter tends to let employers off the hook. In fiscal year 2008, for example, Immigration and Customs Enforcement made over 6,000 work-site enforcement arrests, including over 1,000 criminal arrests.[19] Although these arrests represent a huge increase over work-site enforcement a decade ago, only some 10 percent of the arrests were actually of owners, managers, supervisors, and the like—the bulk were of unauthorized workers themselves.

Millions of undocumented immigrants live and work in the United States, a fact that hints at the difficulty of stemming the inflow of such migrants. As long as jobs are available, the inflow seems likely to continue. Apprehensions along the U.S.-Mexico border began falling precipitously when the construction industry slowed in late 2006 and 2007, and growth in the undocumented workforce came to a complete halt with the onset of the U.S. recession, but no one would argue in favor of slowing the economy in order to end illegal immigration. Workplace enforcement through fast, accurate verification of legal status is the surest means of reducing inflows. But strict enforcement will be most effective and create the least economic disruption if combined with a way for such workers to enter legally. The plan outlined in chapter 3 therefore advocates establishing a legalization program for current unauthorized workers and their dependents and creating a legal means for low-skilled workers to enter in the future.

Why Not End Birthright Citizenship?

Another argument made by some critics of current immigration policy is that the United States should stop automatically awarding U.S. citizenship to anyone born on U.S. soil. The Fourteenth Amendment to the Constitution has consistently been interpreted as granting this right. However, some argue that this policy, called *jus solis*, encourages unauthorized immigrants to have children in the United States in order to establish a toehold in the country.[20] Estimates suggest that there are some four million such children—over 5 percent of the child population—currently in the United States.[21] Because welfare programs treat all U.S. citizens alike, regardless of their parents' citizenship status, these children are eligible for benefits on the same basis as all other citizens. And because their parents are more likely to be poor, welfare eligibility rates are relatively high among such children.[22]

The main alternative to the current *jus solis* policy is *jus sanguinis*, in which citizenship is based solely on parents' citizenship.[23] A *jus sanguinis* policy also can be structured to grant citizenship based on more distant relatives' citizenship, such as a grandparent. Germany and a number of other southern and eastern European countries have traditionally followed the *jus sanguinis* principle.[24] Many countries, including the United States, also grant some people citizenship based on neither place of birth nor parentage but instead on duration of residence and other qualifications, such as language ability or economic contributions.

The United States should not end its policy of birthright citizenship. A *jus sanguinis* policy can create a permanent underclass of children who live their entire lives in one country but are citizens of another. As these children grow into adulthood, they are virtually stateless. They, and their families, have less incentive to integrate into the host country, given that they have fewer rights. In addition, there is little reason to believe that ending birthright citizenship would reduce illegal immigration, which is primarily motivated by jobs. The idea that large numbers of unauthorized immigrants flock to the United States solely to have children who can sponsor their parents for legal residence twenty-one years later is simply absurd. After all, how are those parents supposed to survive in the country until they can obtain legal status? By working. It is better to crack down on employers of undocumented workers and thereby stem the continued flow of such migrants than to create a permanent second class of residents.

Conclusion

Alternatives to the immigration plan proposed in chapter 3 abound. Switching to a point system is perhaps the most common reform urged by proponents of employment-based immigration reform. A point system can be used to attract more high-skilled workers, but it is incompatible with bringing in low-skilled workers. It is also more complex and insensitive to market forces than the auction-based system proposed here. A point-based system substitutes the judgment of government bureaucrats for that of the market.

Other proposals are also problematic. Switching to an open immigration regime is both unlikely and ill-advised. Crafting a NAFTA labor market would put significant pressures on low-skilled native workers' wages and the welfare state. Creating a guest worker program would require figuring out how to ensure that guest workers are not exploited but also return home. An auction system captures the advantages of a guest-worker program without its disadvantages.

Dealing with unauthorized immigration is perhaps the biggest conundrum for immigration reform. Although no solution is perfect, deporting all unauthorized immigrants or ending birthright citizenship would do more harm than good. The former is costly and inhumane, while the latter creates a permanent second class without addressing the jobs magnet, the reason most unauthorized migrants enter. A strict program requiring employer verification of workers' legal status combined with a legal means for bringing in low-skilled foreign workers is the best way to address the problem of continued illegal immigration.

Conclusion: Beyond the Golden Door

In the new era of globalization, the world's best and brightest are on the move, traversing the globe in search of better opportunities. Many want to come to the United States, more than we can accommodate under current law. So we turn high-skilled migrants away, some because they cannot get visas, others because they are discouraged from even trying; still others give up after spending years languishing in long queues. At the same time, high-skilled migrants are increasingly fast-tracked into Canada, the UK, and the EU.

The United States must take advantage of the fact that many of the world's most skilled workers want to come here. As the locus of economic growth shifts to Asia, global workers' ordering of preferred destinations will surely change, and the United States may not come out on top. The country needs to reform immigration policy now. Under current immigration laws, the United States gives 84 percent of permanent resident visas to family-based, diversity, and humanitarian immigrants. No other OECD nation relegates such a peripheral role to employment-based migration, and the United States should not do so either. Employment-based immigrants have higher education, match the economy's needs, and are less likely to be a fiscal burden to taxpayers. They fill crucial gaps in the native workforce in myriad ways, spur innovation and entrepreneurship in the high-tech sector, propel research forward in the life sciences, and staff hospitals and clinics. Increasing the proportion of high-skilled employment-based immigration will benefit current and future generations of Americans.

Untold numbers of low-skilled workers also want to enter the United States. But current policy thwarts most of these potential migrants from entering legally unless they have a close relative already here. Because of country caps, many who do have a relative here must wait decades for a visa. As a result, hundreds of thousands enter illegally in a typical year.

110

Immigration reform needs to recognize that the standard of living in the United States has come to depend in part on low-skilled immigration. Reform should emphasize high-skilled immigration but also allow employers to bring in low-skilled workers on a provisional basis. The United States should create a pathway to permanent residence for legal immigrants who succeed here while cutting off the incentives to migrate illegally.

Our plan prioritizes employment-based immigration but not by simply increasing the number of visas in existing programs. That approach would be a band-aid, not a cure. Increasing temporary nonimmigrant visas, such as H-1B visas, would exacerbate the queues for permanent resident visas, particularly for workers from India and China. In general, creating more visas for existing programs would not resolve queuing or improve how visas are allocated. Under our plan, green cards and other visas will no longer be doled out by lottery or on the basis of first come, first served. Instead, visas will be allocated efficiently—going to the immigrants who add the greatest value and are the most productive—by means of an auction: employers will bid for permits to hire foreign workers, and workers who have passed background checks will then be given provisional work-based visas. This system is designed to maximize the gains to the U.S. economy and admit the best workers, since surely employers will do a better job of selecting immigrants than would government bureaucrats under a point system.

Auction-based permits have several additional benefits. Beyond constituting the best selection mechanism, they allow the government to adjust the number of permits depending on economic circumstances. The government will be able to gauge changes in demand by observing employers' bids at auctions, and it can then adjust supply accordingly, making more permits available during expansions and fewer permits during economic downturns. Using both this timely information about labor demand and the recommendations of an independent commission, the government can allocate an appropriate number of permits to auction off. A secondary market in permits, where employers can sell permits to each other, will also provide information about demand for foreign workers.

Employment-based immigration along with an auction system will therefore provide a selective, flexible, and efficient method of allocating visas. We recommend that separate auctions be created for high-skilled, low-skilled, and seasonal workers so that permit prices can be set independently.

Auctions and tradable permits are preferable to guest-worker programs that tie workers to particular employers and can result in exploitation and abuse.

Yet another advantage of the auction system, and one of the key elements of our plan, is that it captures some of the gains from immigration and redistributes them. A portion of the funds raised by auctioning off permits can be disbursed to offset costs to communities and native workers adversely affected by immigration. These funds will serve other purposes as well: they act as a tax on foreign labor, making domestic workers more desirable; and by reducing the fiscal burdens imposed by immigration, they can decrease political opposition to it.[1]

Under our plan, current unauthorized immigrants are given provisional legal status. There are over eight million such immigrants working here, many with U.S.-born children and deep ties to the United States. To be sure, their work and sacrifices must be weighed against the fact that they have broken the law; the hidden cost of amnesty is the incentive it creates for future illegal immigration. But this problem can be minimized by making amnesty part of comprehensive immigration reform, including provisions for biometric identification cards and electronic verification of immigrants' eligibility to work in the United States.

The plan outlined here mitigates the effect of immigration on natives' labor market outcomes in several ways. Because it raises the price of foreign workers relative to natives, employers have an incentive to hire natives first. The auction system ensures that foreign workers are hired by the sectors that value them the most; this should be sectors that are experiencing labor shortages and are growing. Immigration thus acts as a means of smoothing the business cycle. Natives (and earlier immigrants) may experience smaller wage gains than they would absent foreign workers, but this effect will no longer be concentrated most heavily on the least-skilled and most vulnerable workers. Strict work-site enforcement to keep out unauthorized immigrants will particularly help shield low-skilled workers from adverse impacts.

Who can pass through the golden door? The plan proposed here shifts the focus of immigration from family reunification to employment. With the aging of the American population and heightened global competition for talent, U.S. immigration policy must be redesigned to admit the workers that the economy and society need. The number of immigrants admitted for work-related reasons has been increasing, but these visas are not necessarily allocated efficiently, nor are enough available. Potential immigrants and their employers face binding quotas, and there is overwhelming evidence of unmet demand for high-skilled foreign workers. Family reunification migrants—the bulk of people admitted under the current scheme—do not necessarily have the qualifications that employers require or that will benefit the nation the most. Family reunification also heaps more benefits on a group that already gains the most from immigrating—the immigrants themselves.

Immigration policy can be crafted in any number of ways, so how does a nation decide what is the best policy? What should guide our choices? Certainly the desires of natives—the voters—have to be respected. Clearly the nation's commitments to human rights and to the welfare of its global neighbors have to be maintained. And the lessons of history have to be incorporated. But what should be the ultimate purpose for admitting foreigners through the golden door? That purpose has to be to make our nation stronger. Only such a broad-based principle will rally people in support of immigration reform and create a sustainable system of laws that government agencies will be able to enforce, immigrants will be grateful to benefit from, and natives will be proud to support. In recent years, policymakers have focused almost exclusively on national security. Border enforcement, background checks, and biometric identification cards are a necessary but partial solution. A more complete solution makes use of immigration policy to help secure the nation's economic future.

What is needed is a system that upholds the law; provides and protects the legal means of immigration; and has the courage to address illegal immigration at its source, which is the jobs magnet. The current system needs to be scrapped in favor of one that funnels the most valued foreign workers to the most productive employers in a timely, efficient way and that addresses the core of opposition to immigration by transferring some of the immigration surplus to workers and communities adversely affected by immigration.

What lies beyond the golden door has changed little in the past hundred years. It is the American dream, the promise of a better life for immigrants and their children. What we have increasingly come to understand is that immigrants return the favor through their contributions to the economy and civil society. Immigration policy can be reformed to help safeguard economic opportunities for all citizens and to secure our future prosperity—or a historic opportunity can be squandered. What is needed now is a system that opens the golden door to the immigrants the United States most needs, and leaders with the courage to embark on this new path.

Notes

Introduction

1. Globalization refers to the freer international flow of trade (goods and services), capital, and labor. It is commonly believed that free trade and open immigration characterized the late 1800s and early 1900s in the Americas. But Hatton and Williamson (2005) and references therein explain that, although migration flows were massive and largely unrestricted, trade barriers were actually quite high before World War I. Economic growth, globalized capital markets, and improvements in transportation, not free trade policies themselves, explain the boom in global trade during that period.

2. Hatton and Williamson (1998) show that U.S. economic conditions strongly influenced emigration from European countries during the period 1860 to 1917. Detrended emigration rates for a sample of European countries share the same cyclical pattern, suggesting that short-run variation in emigration rates was driven by conditions in the destination country more than by conditions in the home country.

3. See, for example, Sachs (2008).

4. The foreign born were responsible for 48 percent of labor-force growth between 1996 and 2008, with natives adding 10.5 million and immigrants contributing 9.7 million workers. Authors' calculations based on data from the 1996 and 2008 Current Population Survey, available at http://www.census.gov/cps/.

5. Authors' calculations based on data from the 2007 American Community Survey, available at http://factfinder.census.gov/servlet/DatasetMainPageServlet?_program=ACS&_submenuId=&_lang=en&_ts=. This is an underestimate because it does not include foreign-born persons who arrived after 1990 but have since departed or died.

6. Passel and Cohn (2008b).

7. Passel and Cohn (2008a).

8. Authors' calculations based on data for people age twenty-five and older from the 2007 American Community Survey, available at http://factfinder.census.gov/servlet/DatasetMainPageServlet?_program=ACS&_submenuId=&_lang=en&_ts=.

9. Authors' calculations based on data for people age five and older from the 2007 American Community Survey, ibid.

10. Papademetriou (2005).

11. United Nations Population Fund (2006).

12. United Nations High Commissioner for Refugees (2007). Interestingly, the number of new international migrants has actually declined in recent decades and was smaller during 1990–2005 than during 1975–1990. This decline occurred because of a drop in the number of refugees.

13. Rodrik (2005).

14. There are also tremendous cultural, psychological, and social barriers to migration, such as the desire to live near family and people who share the same language and culture. Many people would not want to migrate even if pecuniary migration costs were zero. This book views migration from an economic perspective. For a broader discussion of sociological and economic perspectives on migration, see, for example, Portes (1995) and Massey et al. (1999).

15. See, for example, Rodrik (2001), Pritchett (2006), and Hatton (2007).

Chapter 1: The Challenge: Picking Up the Pieces

1. For a more detailed history of U.S. immigration policy, see, for example, chapter 2 of Smith and Edmonston (1997); Tichenor (2002); and Daniels (2004).

2. Passel and Cohn (2009).

3. Daniels (2004).

4. In 1929, revised national origin quotas based on the 1920 census went into effect, and total immigration from the Eastern Hemisphere (effectively Europe, since immigration from most Asian nations was still barred) was limited to about 150,000 people annually. Interestingly, these quotas left immigration from the Western Hemisphere completely unrestricted. Apparently, immigration from that region was small enough—particularly in comparison to inflows from southern and eastern Europe—not to trigger concerns.

5. Daniels (2004, 120).

6. Smith and Edmonston (1997).

7. Statistics on Mexican immigration are from table 2 of U.S. Department of Homeland Security (2009b).

8. Mora-Torres (2001).

9. Massey, Durand, and Malone (2002).

10. Unauthorized Mexican migration also was a problem during the *bracero* period, however. For example, Border Patrol made over half a million apprehensions during FY 1951, almost all of Mexicans trying to illegally enter the United States. U.S. Immigration and Naturalization Service (1951).

11. The estimates of illegal immigration are from Massey and Singer (1995). The statistic on legal permanent residents is the authors' calculation from INS Statistical Yearbooks during that period.

12. Hoefer (1991).

13. Before the bars, illegal immigrants who had entered without inspection but had since become eligible for permanent residence could leave the United States and apply for adjustment of status at a U.S. consulate. The admissibility bars prevented their reentry, largely ending this practice. INA section 245(i) provided temporary reprieve to such immigrants by allowing them to file inside the United States after paying a $1,000 fine. This provision of the law was in effect only between 1994 and 1998 and for the first few months of 2001.

14. Many of IIRIRA's provisions were not fully implemented until the 9/11 terrorist attacks. In 2002, the student database became SEVIS (the Student and Exchange Visitor Information System); in 2004, the entry-exit system became U.S. Visit.

15. However, these restrictions are being chipped away over time because of legal challenges, states choosing to restore some benefits, and the federal government reversing some of its earlier decisions. See Hanson et al. (2002) for a discussion.

16. The House passed H.R. 4437 in December 2005. The Border Protection, Antiterrorism and Illegal Immigration Control Act of 2005 consisted largely of enforcement measures meant to curb immigration; it mandated the construction of a U.S.-Mexico border fence, for example, and got rid of the diversity visa program. Most notably, H.R. 4437 made the most common federal immigration offenses (such as illegal presence) aggravated felonies for the purposes of immigration law. Noncitizens convicted of aggravated felonies are immediately deportable and ineligible for any reprieve, such as cancellation of removal. As a result, H.R. 4437 was completely incompatible with the amnesty and passage of the Senate bill and meant there could be no compromise with the Senate on a comprehensive immigration reform bill. The immigrant community's outrage over the House bill sparked widespread protests.

17. The 2006 version of the AgJOBS Act conferred "blue card" status upon farm workers who had worked in agriculture in the United States for at least 863 hours or 150 workdays during a twenty-four-month period. AgJOBS would allow blue-card aliens (and their spouses and minor children) to adjust to permanent resident status after three to five additional years of agricultural employment. The Development, Relief and Education for Alien Minors Act (DREAM Act) would provide the opportunity to earn conditional permanent residency to certain immigrant students who graduated from U.S. high schools, were of good moral character, had arrived in the country as children, and had been in the country continuously for at least five years prior to the bill's enactment. The students would obtain temporary residency for six years, during which time they had to attend college and earn a two-year degree or serve a two-year stint in the military in order to eventually earn a green card.

18. By the time the federal rule became law, eleven states had already passed legislation requiring certain employers to participate in E-Verify.

19. About 43 percent of accompanying spouses ("derivatives") of principals granted an employment-based green card in fiscal year 2000 reported their occupation

as homemaker. About 3 percent reported being students and 5 percent being unemployed. Another 26 percent did not report an occupation. This suggests that over three-quarters of these spouses are not in the labor force. Authors' calculations based on the FY 2000 Legal Immigration Public Use File for married persons age eighteen and older (U.S. Immigration and Naturalization Service 2002).

20. The data refer to immigrants age twenty-five and older and only to the principal and spouse (not accompanying dependents). See Jasso et al. (2000).

21. The H-2B returning worker exemption, in effect during 2005–2007, allowed workers who had been counted against the H-2B cap in the three previous years to reenter the United States to work for the same seasonal employer without counting against the cap.

22. Canadians do not require visas to enter the United States, so they receive TN "authorization," not a TN visa. Figure 1-6 shows the combined number of TN visas and authorizations.

23. Estimates from U.S. Department of Homeland Security (2010) put the undocumented population at 10.8 million in January 2009, down from 11.6 million a year earlier. The Pew Hispanic Center estimated there were 11.9 million undocumented immigrants living in the United States in March 2008; see Passel and Cohn (2008a). Estimates of the number of undocumented immigrants draw on surveys of the general population to estimate the total number of foreign-born persons and then subtract estimates of the legally present foreign born, which are calculated from temporary and permanent visa issuances and admissions. Entries of illegal immigrants have slowed with the economy since 2006 or 2007, but the vast majority of unauthorized immigrants appear to have remained in the country even during the recession that began in late 2007.

24. See, for example, Hanson and Spilimbergo (1999), Orrenius (1999), and Orrenius and Zavodny (2005).

25. See, for example, Fortuny, Capps, and Passel (2007).

26. See Congressional Budget Office (2007b) and references therein.

27. Although the absolute number of the foreign born is much larger in the United States than elsewhere, a few smaller countries, in particular Canada and Australia, have higher immigration rates relative to their population. United Nations Department of Economic and Social Affairs (2006) estimates that the United States had over thirty-eight million international migrants in 2005 (13 percent of its total population), compared with four million (24 percent) in Australia and six million (19 percent) in Canada. The United Kingdom had five million international migrants (9 percent of its population).

28. For example, Germany and Sweden offer generous welfare payments to asylum seekers and refugees but restrict their ability to work. Brücker et al. (2002).

29. OECD (2008). Brücker et al. (2002) and Orrenius and Solomon (2006) also discuss immigrant-native unemployment rate differences across countries.

30. See the discussions in Brücker et al. (2002) and Orrenius and Solomon (2006).

31. For permanent visas, the figure shows the number of employment-based visas issued for the first, second, and third employment preference classes, not including spouses and children, other workers, or beneficiaries of the Chinese Student Adjustment Act. This is somewhat of an undercount of skilled workers, since the spouses, who are eligible to work, also may be skilled workers. It does not include special workers or investors. The temporary work visa categories included besides H-1B are TN authorizations and visas, which allow skilled immigration from Canada and Mexico; L visas for intracompany transfers; and O1 visas for persons of extraordinary ability. E1 and E2 visas for businessmen and investors likely accounted for at least another twelve thousand visas or so in 2008 but are not included here because spouses and children cannot be subtracted from the total in the published data.

32. E, L, H-1B, and O visas do not require temporary (non-immigrant) intent, and so adjustment of status is fairly straightforward, given an employer who will sponsor the petition. This is not the case for TN visas.

33. U.S. Citizenship and Immigration Services (2010).

34. The general trend over the last decade has been improving employers' access to foreign workers through temporary visa programs. However, there have been recent setbacks. New rules governing H-2A visas that went into effect March 15, 2010, require documented recruitment of U.S. workers, higher wages, and stricter safety provisions. In 2008, the Troubled Asset Relief Program (TARP) subjected banks and financial institutions receiving federal bailout funds to tougher rules on hiring foreign workers through the H-1B program.

35. These changes were part of the American Competitiveness in the Twenty-First Century Act of 2000. An H-1B holder now can move to a new job as soon as the new employer files an H-1B petition for the worker; previously, visa holders had to wait for approval before switching employers. H-1B holders with an approved employment-based immigrant petition (Form I-140) can change jobs or employers if an application to adjust status (Form I-485) is filed and unadjudicated for 180 days and the new position is similar to the position for which the original petition was filed. See U.S. Citizenship and Immigration Service (2008a).

36. U.S. Department of State (2009b).

37. See table 6 of U.S. Department of Homeland Security (2009b). Excluding refugees and asylees, family-based admissions are almost 80 percent of permanent resident visas.

38. However, as discussed in box 2-1 in chapter 2, skill-based immigration may not benefit the source country if it results in a large-scale brain drain.

39. Authors' calculation based on data from the March 2008 Current Population Survey (http://www.census.gov/cps/) for program benefit receipt during 2007. Means-tested welfare programs include public assistance (Temporary Assistance for Needy Families, or TANF); means-tested health insurance (via Medicaid or State Children's Health Insurance Program, or SCHIP); Supplemental Security Income (SSI); benefits through the Women, Infants, and Children (WIC) program; public

housing or rental assistance; food stamps; energy assistance; and free or reduced-price lunch for schoolchildren. Among household heads who do not have a high school diploma, the welfare program participation rate was 55 percent for immigrants and 44 percent for natives; for heads who do not have a bachelor's degree, it was 42 percent for immigrants and 25 percent for natives.

40. Wadhwa, Jasso et al. (2007).

41. See Park (2007) and Jasso (2009) for a discussion of this point. Spouses of F-1 student visa holders (who hold an F-2 visa), spouses of M-1 vocational students (who hold an M-2 visa), and spouses of O-1 and P visa workers (who hold O-3 and P-4 visas) also are unable to work.

42. Authors' calculations based on table 9 of Department of Homeland Security (2009b) data on people obtaining legal permanent resident status in FY 2008. About 58 percent of family-based immigrants (immediate relatives and family-sponsored immigrants) were female versus 48 percent of employment-based immigrants; 8 percent were age 65 or older (versus less than 1 percent); and 10 percent reported being unemployed (versus 2 percent).

43. Based on U.S. Department of State (2009a).

44. In addition, the quota can be exceeded because of "recapture," in which employment-based visas that went unused in previous years are made available in later years. Recapture requires a specific act of Congress; it is not automatic or at the discretion of the executive branch. Recapture legislation was passed most recently in 2005. Employment-based visas have gone unused in some years, not because of lack of demand for them but because of lags in processing.

45. See U.S. Citizenship and Immigration Service (2008b). The 85,000 visas is the total of 65,000 plus the additional 20,000 currently available to holders of a U.S. advanced degree. The cap was reached even in FY 2010, although it did take almost nine months to hit the quota in the depths of the "Great Recession." This occurred not only despite the downturn but also despite restrictions on hiring H-1Bs imposed on financial services firms that accepted bailout funds from the federal government.

46. Of course, lotteries may be justified on non-economic grounds, such as fairness.

47. These criticisms aside, it should be noted that the diversity program brings in more highly skilled immigrants than does family-based immigration. Because diversity visa holders must either have a high school diploma or equivalent or meet certain work experience requirements, these immigrants are relatively skilled. According to Jasso et al. (2000), data from the 1996 pilot of the New Immigrant Survey indicate that new recipients of diversity visas had 14.7 mean years of education, versus 12.7 for all new green card holders. Diversity visa immigrants also tend to be in relatively high-paid occupations compared with family-sponsored immigrants; see Barrett (1996).

48. Authors' calculations based on data for individuals in the labor force age twenty-five and older from 1996 and 2008 Current Population Survey, available at http://www.census.gov/cps/.

49. See, for example, Eschbach et al. (1999) and Massey, Durand, and Malone (2002).
50. See Office of Management and Budget (2007, 2008).
51. Carrion-Flores and Sorensen (2009).
52. Angelucci (2005), Reyes (2004), and Riosmena (2004).
53. See Orrenius and Zavodny (2009).

Chapter 2: The Goal: Pro-Growth Immigration Policy

1. As discussed in the previous chapter, efforts at immigration policy reform were derailed in 2006 and 2007 largely by public concern that, like earlier reform efforts, they would fail to stem the flow of unauthorized migrants. An immigration policy that puts developing countries on an equal footing with the United States and other rich countries would generate such massive migrant flows as to be truly unacceptable to most of the American public. A theoretical model and simulation developed by Benhabib and Jovanovic (2007) shows that if the welfare of people in all countries is weighted equally, up to 3.2 billion people should migrate from developing to developed countries.

2. Pritchett (2006) provides an accessible overview of moral arguments about immigration policy from an economist's perspective. He concludes that rich countries should allow much freer labor migration.

3. For a good summary of the possible effects of international migration on sending countries, see, for example, chapter 3 of World Bank (2006a). For an overview of research on brain drain, see Commander, Kangasniemi, and Winters (2004).

4. Rosenzweig (2007).

5. Docquier and Rapoport (2009).

6. The discussion of globalization policies and trends in recent economic history draws heavily on Wynne (2009).

7. The price of a ten-minute international phone call fell from one thousand work-hours in 1934 to less than one-tenth of a work-hour in 2004; see Federal Reserve Bank of Dallas (2006). Ad valorem shipping costs declined from 10 percent in 1974 to 6 percent in 2004 for ocean freight and from 13 percent to 8 percent for air freight over the same period. Hummels (2007).

8. Lane and Milesi-Ferretti (2006).

9. Ibid.

10. Trade statistics are from U.S. Census Bureau (2010); for Chinese concerns, see Batson and Browne (2009).

11. Hatton and Williamson (1998).

12. Clemens, Montenegro, and Pritchett (2008).

13. Hanson (2008) and Rosenzweig (2007).

14. World Bank (2008).

15. Part of the increase in formal remittances is due to better measurement and a shift from informal transfers to formal remittances. See World Bank (2006b).

16. Ratha (2007).

17. Many people are reluctant to move for reasons related to cultural factors or family ties. The pecuniary gains from migration would need to be even larger to induce such people to move.

18. See chapter 4 of Smith and Edmonston (1997) for a detailed explanation and estimates of the immigration surplus. For other estimates of the immigration surplus, see, for example, Borjas (1999a) and Council of Economic Advisers (2007).

19. This discussion relies on chapter 9 in Bodvarsson and Van den Berg (2009).

20. Hunt and Gauthier-Lauselle (2008) find that immigrants patent at double the rate of natives. This difference is explained by immigrants' overrepresentation in science and engineering. They find some evidence of positive spillovers on natives. Kerr and Lincoln (2008) find that increases in H-1B (temporary skilled worker visas) admissions significantly raise patent activity by people with Indian and Chinese names without reducing (and perhaps even increasing) patent activity by people with English names. Hunt (2009) finds that, among college graduates, immigrants are more likely to have been granted a patent than natives. The difference is due to immigrants admitted on temporary work visas and on student visas. Chellaraj, Maskus, and Mattoo (2005) also report positive effects of foreign graduate students and immigrants on patents.

21. Hunt (2009) concludes that, among college graduates, immigrants are more likely to have started a business than natives. The Small Business Administration (2008) reports that immigrants are nearly 30 percent more likely to start a business than natives.

22. Wadhwa, Gereffi et al. (2007).

23. The seminal work on selection among immigrants is Borjas (1987). Borjas presents a theoretical model for why immigrants are positively selected from countries with lower returns to skill (less income inequality) than the United States. This characterizes most of the European and Asian countries that are major sources of skilled immigrants. See also Chiswick (1999). Borjas's predictions are not borne out, however, with respect to negative selection of immigrants from poor countries with high degrees of income inequality, such as Mexico. Chiquiar and Hanson (2005) and Orrenius and Zavodny (2005) conclude that immigration from Mexico tends to come from the middle of the skill distribution. In addition, Borjas and Bratsberg (1996) show that when immigrants are positively selected, the process of return migration intensifies the positive selection (among the skilled migrants who come, the least skilled will return home).

24. See, for example, Kerr (2008).

25. Commission on Professionals in Science and Technology (2005).

26. Authors' calculations from Current Population Survey data for 2003 to 2008, available at http://www.census.gov/cps/.

27. Saxenian and Shin (2006).

28. Porter (1998).

29. Glaeser and Saiz (2003).

30. Schumpeter (1934).

31. Mokyr (1990), Holmes and Schmitz (1994, 1998), and Bodvarsson and Van den Berg (2009).

32. Tiebout (1956) discusses labor mobility in response to public policy, and Lucas (1990) discusses capital flows more broadly. The importance of public policy and institutions is underscored by the World Bank (2006b) report which finds that intangible capital is the largest component of national wealth. Intangible capital includes institutions, such as the rule of law, and human capital.

33. Cortes and Tessada (2008) and Furtado and Hock (2008).

34. Lewis (2005) and Martin (2007).

35. Saiz (2007). See also Hoover Institution (1997) and Millman (1997).

36. Bodvarsson, Van den Berg, and Lewer (2008).

37. U.S. Bureau of the Census (2003) and Bean et al. (2007).

38. Smith and Edmonston (1997).

39. For example, Card (2001) estimates that immigrant inflows in the late 1980s reduced the wages of low-skilled workers by at most 3 percent. Orrenius and Zavodny (2007) report that inflows of immigrants in low-skilled occupations reduced wages of natives in those occupations by about 0.8 percent during 1994–2000, while inflows of immigrants in medium- and high-skilled occupations did not significantly affect wages of natives in those occupations. Ottaviano and Peri (2008) estimate that immigrant inflows during 1990–2006 appear to have reduced wages of workers who did not have a high school diploma by about 0.7 percent in the short run but will raise them by 0.3 percent in the long run. For surveys of the literature, see Friedberg and Hunt (1995) and Borjas (1999a); for a meta-analysis, see Longhi, Nijkamp, and Poot (2005). For estimates of wage effects that are more negative, see, for example, Borjas, Grogger, and Hanson (2008) and Borjas (2003). Borjas (2003) concludes that immigration lowered average native wages by 3.2 percent between 1980 and 2000, with the estimated effect ranging from 8.9 percent for workers without a high school diploma to almost no effect among workers with some college education but not a bachelor's degree.

40. See, for example, DiNardo, Fortin, and Lemieux (1996) for a discussion of institutional factors like unions and the minimum wage; see Goldin and Katz (2007) for a discussion of skill-based technological change. International trade or "globalization" does not appear to have played a large role in the decline in low-skilled workers' earnings during 1960–1990. Borjas, Freeman, and Katz (1997).

41. Ottaviano and Peri (2008) estimate that immigrant inflows during 1990–2006 reduced the wages of previous immigrants by about 5–8 percent, depending on their level of education.

42. Bodvarsson, Van den Berg, and Lewer (2008).

43. Borjas and Katz (2007) find no effect of immigration on average native wages in the long run for this reason.

44. Some research suggests that this contribution has been relatively modest. Card (2009) concludes that immigration can explain about 5 percent of the rise in overall wage inequality between 1980 and 2000. Because wage measures include only workers with positive earnings (and thus do not capture any negative employment effects), the effect on income inequality is likely to be larger than the effect on wages.

45. We focus here on fiscal costs directly related to immigration. However, immigration also may impose fiscal costs indirectly via adverse labor market effects on natives. If some natives experience lower employment rates and earnings as a result of immigrant inflows, their eligibility for government transfer programs may increase. We are not aware of any research directly on this issue.

46. Research suggests that 80 percent of children of immigrant parents (and 73 percent of children of undocumented immigrant parents) are U.S. citizens. See Capps and Fortuny (2006) and Passel and Cohn (2009).

47. Smith and Edmonston (1997).

48. Ibid .

49. It bears repeating that illegal immigrants are not eligible for welfare programs, nor can they access unemployment, disability, and retirement benefits. For estimates of fiscal costs of illegal immigration, see Congressional Budget Office (2007b).

50. Smith and Edmonston (1997).

51. As noted in the beginning of this chapter, we are taking a U.S.-centric view. A more complete accounting of the gains to immigration that includes the immigrants themselves would be overwhelmingly positive.

52. OECD (2009a).

53. This box draws on OECD (2008).

54. See Hatton (2007) for a discussion.

55. Hanson (2009).

56. Bulgaria and Romania joined in 2007; Cyprus, the Czech Republic, Estonia, Hungary, Latvia, Lithuania, Malta, Poland, Slovakia, and Slovenia joined in 2004.

57. An annual cap of 5,500 TN visas for skilled Mexican workers was removed in 2004 (Orrenius and Streitfeld 2006).

58. See, for example, Hanson (2005) and Scheve and Slaughter (2001).

59. See Karoly and Panis (2009) for a discussion of this point.

60. The future does not look brighter. The Programme for International Student Assessment ranks the United States twenty-fourth of twenty-eight developed countries on mean student performance among fifteen-year-olds. Karoly and Panis (2009).

61. See Martin, Lowell, and Bump (2009) and National Research Council (2009).

62. Bound, Turner, and Walsh (2009).

63. It is still important to condition work visas for foreign students on offers of employment. Unconditional visas for foreign students upon graduation from U.S. universities could lead to excessive enrollment and unemployment among graduates.

64. See Karoly and Panis (2009) and U.S. Bureau of Labor Statistics (2009).

65. For research about the effects of immigration on prices, see, for example, chapter 5 of Smith and Edmonston (1997) and Cortes (2008).

66. Immigration policy reform cannot be used to maintain the age structure of the U.S. labor force (as opposed to help address the needs created by an aging population). Freeman (2006) indicates that stabilizing the U.S. age structure would require that some 10.8 million immigrants enter annually, more than an order of magnitude greater than current inflows. For details on the aging of the U.S. workforce, see U.S. Department of Labor (2004).

67. The Bureau of Labor Statistics projects that between 2006 and 2016, at least ten of the twenty fastest-growing occupations will relate to health care, including the second- and third-fastest growing occupations (personal and home care aides and home health aides, respectively). See U.S. Bureau of Labor Statistics (2009). The fastest-growing category is network systems and data communications analysts, pointing to the continued need for skilled IT workers. Looking at growth levels instead of rates, registered nurses comprise the fastest-growing occupation, with personal and home care aides ranked sixth and home health aides ranked seventh.

68. Hatton and Williamson (1998).

69. See Piore (1979).

70. See Mayr and Peri (2008) and OECD (2008). Earlier estimates from the 1960s and 1970s indicate slightly higher return migration rates; see Borjas and Bratsberg (1996), Jasso and Rosenzweig (1982), and Warren and Peck (1980).

71. Congressional Research Service (2007) indicates that about one-half of H-1B workers adjust to permanent resident status.

72. Most visas still require that the holder not intend to remain permanently in the United States (not have "immigrant intent"). Some visas, including H-1B and L-1, now allow holders to apply for permanent resident status while present in the United States under the "dual intent" rule; these visa holders are classified as nonimmigrants but may decide in the future to seek permanent residence. The dual intent provision does not apply to student visas or tourist visas, among many other categories.

73. Saxenian (2006) and Zweig (2007).

74. Official remittance flows are estimated to have totaled $305 billion in 2008; see Ratha and Mohapatra (2009). For studies on the importance and economics of remittances, see, for example, the studies in Fajnzylber and López (2008) and Rapoport and Docquier (2006).

75. Labor market testing is required for EB-2 and EB-3 immigrants in the form of labor certification, and for H-1B workers through labor condition applications and employer attestations. There are similar requirements for the H-2A and H-2B programs. Labor certification or attestation is not required for some foreign workers, such as those in shortage occupations or with exceptional skills.

76. For example, 99.7 percent of labor condition applications submitted electronically as supporting evidence for H-1B petitions in fiscal year 2008 were certified.

Authors' calculations from data available at Foreign Labor Certification Data Center, Online Wage Library, http://www.flcdatacenter.com/CaseH1B.aspx.

77. Of course, unauthorized immigrants tend to come and stay only if they can find work, a different form of labor market testing than the formal process the government requires in order to reduce adverse effects on competing workers.

78. See Smith and Edmonston (1997).

79. See Jasso et al. (2000), Ku (2006), and Mohanty et al. (2005).

80. Passel and Suro (2005).

Chapter 3: The Way: Market-Based Immigration Reform

1. On the potential migrant side, there is likely to be considerable excess demand for provisional work visas. But there would be no official queue guaranteeing people a right to immigrate in the future as there is today. Employers would presumably have a large pool of foreign workers from which to choose. The current H-2A and H-2B programs offer an example of how this process would likely work on the low-skilled side—employers might simply hire back their old workers or contract with recruiting agencies to help them screen potential workers. Skilled workers would probably largely continue to be foreign graduates of U.S. universities.

2. This permit requirement also does not apply to two types of provisional visa workers discussed below: foreigners in the legal permanent resident queue when reform is implemented, and unauthorized immigrants who qualify for legalization, both of whom are granted provisional visas under the plan proposed here. As we will indicate, those provisional work visa holders can work for any employer; the high-skilled, low-skilled, and seasonal permit system does not apply to them.

3. FICA contributions are currently 15.3 percent of compensation for most workers, with 7.65 percent taken directly from workers' paychecks and the other 7.65 percent paid directly by the employer. But this even split is not the true economic incidence of the tax because of differences in bargaining power and the relative elasticities of labor supply and demand. If foreign workers are refunded their half of the FICA contributions, then the employer probably would be able to reduce the amount that a foreign worker is paid by about that much.

4. Strict enforcement can forestall a race to the bottom by employers of low-skilled workers, as explained in Brown, Hotchkiss, and Quispe-Agnoli (2009).

5. For details, see the Web site of the U.S. Department of Labor, Employment and Training Administration, at http://www.foreignlaborcert.doleta.gov/wages.cfm.

6. As with standard analysis of tax incidence, the party with more inelastic demand or supply bears the bulk of the tax burden.

7. This would be a tax imposed by the United States, not a tax imposed by the source country on its citizens living and working abroad. The latter tax, sometimes termed the "Bhagwati tax," can be a way for source countries to alleviate problems

associated with brain drain. For a discussion, see, for example, Bhagwati (1976). For an example of a U.S. tax on immigrants' income, see Chiswick (1982).

8. This type of tax can also act as an insurance mechanism. Paying a proportional or progressive tax after income is earned reduces risk for immigrants and their employers compared to a fixed fee that is paid up front. If an immigrant earns less than expected, he pays less in taxes.

9. An income tax also is complicated by issues of family labor supply—should the tax apply only to the head of household or to all accompanying dependents who work? If an immigrant marries a native, does the native have to pay the extra tax also or does the couple then have an incentive to shift labor supply to the lower-taxed spouse? The complications seem endless, and the plan would require yet another layer of government involvement above and beyond what is required for the plan proposed here.

10. The federal government can achieve a fairly accurate count of the number of new legal immigrants who work by matching immigration records with Social Security and tax records. We are not aware of any published statistics based on this.

11. Based on 2003 employment rates as reported in Public Policy Institute of California (2008).

12. Based on Passel and Cohn (2009).

13. Of course, legalization also could decrease labor force participation by increasing earnings for newly legalized families (that is, the income effect could dominate the substitution effect).

14. The $3,320 fee to USCIS is based on the $320 filing fee, $1,500 training fee assessed on large employers (which is reduced to $750 for employers with fewer than twenty-five full-time workers), a $500 fraud prevention and detection fee for new petitions or to switch employers, and the optional $1,000 premium processing fee.

15. See, for example, Times Online, "Risking Death Crossing the Mexican Border," January 16, 2009, http://women.timesonline.co.uk/tol/life_and_style/women/the_way_we_live/article5525553.ece. As in other markets, the price of a coyote changes with supply and demand; it rose during the construction boom of the mid-2000s and then fell as the housing bubble burst.

16. Not disclosing the reserve price at the high end is the one violation of transparency we recommend. This is necessary to prevent participants from manipulating the system in order to increase the number of permits issued.

17. See the discussion in Migration Policy Institute (2006) and Papademetriou et al. (2009) on potential structures and functions of a standing commission.

18. Many other rules could be created for setting the number of permits and reserve prices. Changes in wages and the unemployment rate could be used in a manner analogous to the Taylor rule for monetary policy, for example. Transparency is important so that market participants have full information and stable expectations.

19. As discussed in chapter 1, the structure of the current system makes the inflow of immigrants quite insensitive to economic conditions. Caps prevent immigration

inflows from increasing when labor demand is high; when labor demand is low, the lengthy queues for family-preference visas and for most categories of employment-based permanent resident visas, combined with the relatively low caps on temporary work visas, mean that immigration inflows do not slow much.

20. For an excellent introduction to auction design, see Klemperer (2002) or Milgrom (1989).

21. This would be akin to noncompetitive bids in auctions of Treasury securities, where bidders specify the quantity they are willing to purchase at the market price. If the number of these noncompetitive bids by smaller firms exceeds the number of permits set aside for small firms, a lottery could be held to determine who gets to purchase the permits.

22. See Becker (1987), Chiswick (1982), Freeman (2006), Hanson (2009), and Simon (1989). Zimmermann (2009) similarly suggests that EU countries consider auctioning off work permits and entry visas.

23. If policymakers want to continue to admit parents of U.S. citizens, they might consider the Australian model, which requires that parents be aged and have at least one-half of their children living legally and permanently in Australia. See Australian Department of Immigration and Citizenship, "Fact Sheet 31—Family Stream Migration: Parent Category Visas," http://www.immi.gov.au/media/fact-sheets/31parents.htm. This or other hardship criteria could be used to limit the number of parents allowed to enter. We thank an anonymous referee for bringing Australia's program to our attention.

24. See table 6 of U.S. Department of Homeland Security (2009b).

25. See ibid.

26. See Jasso et al. (2000).

27. Under current law, green card holders are allowed to work even if they enter as a dependent (unlike dependents of many temporary work visas). The plan thus would have little impact on their labor force participation.

28. Wadhwa, Jasso et al. (2007).

29. Passel (2005) estimates that there were some 1 million to 1.5 million people with "quasi" legal status present in the United States and waiting for a green card as of March 2005. This includes people with temporary protected status or extended voluntary departure status, asylum seekers, NACARA beneficiaries, and 245(i) applicants. The exact size of the 245(i) pool is not known, but it has been estimated to be between two hundred thousand and three hundred thousand See Congressional Research Service (2002) and Migration Dialogue (2002).

30. Realistically, there is no way to completely eliminate all employment of unauthorized workers, particularly in private households and at day labor sites. Doing so would require something akin to a police state and also would be economically inefficient.

31. Bansak and Raphael (2001) and Lowell, Teachman, and Jing (1995).

32. Belief in the rule of law and public support for immigration reform should be included as gains.

33. Estimates by the Congressional Budget Office and the Joint Committee on Taxation indicate that the legalization programs included in the 2006 and 2007 immigration reform proposals discussed in chapter 2 would have generated billions more in revenue than in additional costs from Social Security, Medicare, refundable tax credits, and other government programs. See U.S. Congressional Budget Office (2006, 2007a).

34. Kossoudji and Cobb-Clark (2002) estimate that legalized workers' earnings rose by about 6 percent for the first three years after IRCA. Rivera-Batiz (1999) finds evidence of even larger effects over the first four years after legalization. In contrast, Hill, Lofstrom, and Hayes (2010) find no effect of legalization on the wages of unauthorized immigrants who had crossed the border illegally, but do find significant positive effects on immigrants who had overstayed visas. Kandilov and Kandilov (2009) find that legalization increases the likelihood of having employer-sponsored health insurance by nine percentage points, a sizable effect.

35. The Comprehensive Immigration Reform Act of 2006 (S. 2611) and 2007 (S. 1348 and S.1639).

36. Authors' calculations based on data from the 2005 to 2007 American Community Survey, available at http://factfinder.census.gov/servlet/DatasetMainPageServlet?_program=ACS&_submenuId=&_lang=en&_ts=. Data specific to education levels include only people age twenty-five and older.

37. Authors' calculations based on data from the 2005 to 2007 American Community Survey, ibid.

38. Ibid. Children includes people age seventeen and younger.

39. See chapter 6 in Smith and Edmonston (1997).

Chapter 4: What the Plan Does Not Include and Why

1. See, for example, Borjas (1999b).

2. See, for example, Antecol, Cobb-Clark, and Trejo (2003) and references therein.

3. See Antecol, Cobb-Clark, and Trejo (2003) and Jasso and Rosenzweig (2009). The latter argue that the immigrants admitted under Australia's point system are similar to those admitted under employment-based preferences in the United States, controlling for differences in the return to skill across the two countries. They conclude, "There is no evidence that the differences in the selection mechanism used to screen employment migrants in the two countries play a significant role in affecting the characteristics of skill migration" (p. 182). However, Chiswick, Le, and Miller (2008) note that the lowest-earning immigrants fare better relative to natives in Australia than in the United States, possibly because of the difference in immigration selection regimes. Chiswick and Miller (2008) conclude that the different immigration selection regimes in the United States and Australia do not affect immigrants' ability to transfer human capital, suggesting that regimes may be trumped by other factors.

4. Papademetriou et al. (2008) show that, for the Australian case, employer-nominated immigrants have lower unemployment rates and higher labor force participation rates than points-tested, skill-based immigrants. Jasso and Rosenzweig (2009) indicate that 11 percent of Australian employment immigrants were unemployed when surveyed, versus less than 5 percent of new (nonadjusting) employment immigrants in the United States. Of course, they note that this difference may reflect differences in labor market conditions, not just in immigration policies, between the two countries. Miller and Neo (2003) suggest that unemployment rates are higher among immigrants in Australia, particularly soon after arrival, than in the United States because wages are more inflexible in Australia.

5. For example, Aydemir and Skuterud (2005) and references therein show that immigrants to Canada have lower returns to education and experience than Canadian natives, indicating less than perfect skill transferability there. Chiswick and Miller (2008) conclude that immigrants to Australia experience limited transferability of their human capital, much like immigrants to the United States and despite the difference in immigrant selection regimes. See Banerjee (2008) and references therein for a discussion of discrimination against minority immigrants in Canada.

6. See note 4 of this chapter.

7. Picot, Hou, and Coulombe (2007).

8. Chapter 9 of Isbister (1996) provides an accessible overview of ethical arguments regarding immigration policies.

9. Friedman made this comment in a number of contexts, including Friedman (1998, 2006).

10. Aydemir and Borjas (2007), Hanson (2007), and Mishra (2007) all report that out-migration from Mexico has raised wages there.

11. Massey, Durand, and Malone (2002) make the case for a NAFTA labor market.

12. The TN visa and authorization numbers give some idea of prospective scale. In FY 2008, the United States admitted about eighty-eight thousand professional workers under the TN provisions; see U.S. Department of State, Report of the Visa Office (various years), http://www.travel.state.gov/visa/frvi/statistics/statistics_1476.html. Fewer than eleven thousand people—a number that includes both workers and accompanying dependents—from Canada received permanent resident visas under employment-based preferences in FY 2008; see U.S. Department of Homeland Security (2009b), table 11. In 2007, there were 831 economic (permanent) immigrants and 17,054 temporary workers to Canada from the United States; see Citizenship and Immigration Canada (2008). Interestingly, while NAFTA devised a skilled visa for Mexican and Canadian professionals, it did nothing to provide for the legal movement of low-skilled or undocumented workers.

13. Hatton and Williamson (2009) argue that demographic changes in Latin America will reduce emigration rates from those countries to the United States by twenty-one to twenty-two log points in the coming decades. They project this effect

will be somewhat offset by changes in poverty rates and other factors but will nonetheless lead to a decline in the immigration rate from that region.

14. See OECD (2009b) and Index Mundi data on Mexican fertility rates at http://www.indexmundi.com/mexico/total_fertility_rate.html (accessed July 1, 2009).

15. See Heisler (2002).

16. See "Braceros: Lost Savings?" *Rural Migration News* 7, no. 2 (April 2001), http://migration.ucdavis.edu/rmn/more.php?id=508_0_4_0.

17. See, for example, Web sites such as VDARE.com and Illegal Aliens.US.

18. Goyle and Jaeger (2005).

19. U.S. Immigration and Customs Enforcement (2009).

20. Such children are sometimes called "anchor babies." See, for example, Federation for American Immigration Reform, "Anchor Babies: Part of the Immigration-Related American Lexicon," http://www.fairus.org/site/PageServer?pagename=iic_immigrationissuecenters4608. Children must be twenty-one years old before they can sponsor their parents (and any foreign-born siblings) for legal permanent residence, implying that such families are extremely far-sighted or patient. Moreover, unless the beneficiary can get a waiver or had applied under section 245(i), adjustment of status will require leaving the country, after which attempted reentry into the United States will trigger the three- or ten-year bar.

21. There are another estimated 1.5 million unauthorized immigrant children in the United States. Passel and Cohn (2009).

22. However, actual take-up is lower among such mixed-status families, in part because of language barriers and parental concerns about deportation.

23. The United States actually has both *jus solis* and *jus sanguine* provisions for awarding citizenship. Children born abroad with a U.S. citizen parent are eligible for U.S. citizenship at birth as long as the parent has met certain U.S. residence requirements.

24. In 1999, Germany passed a new citizenship law that facilitates the naturalization of long-term legal immigrants and grants *jus solis* citizenship to children born in Germany if their parents have legally resided in Germany for at least eight years. These children must later choose between German citizenship and their parents' citizenship (Heisler 2002).

Conclusion: Beyond the Golden Door

1. Scheve and Slaughter (2007) make the same argument that redistributing the gains from trade can help reduce opposition to free trade agreements, while Hanson (2009) makes a similar argument about immigration.

References

Angelucci, Manuela. 2005. U.S. border enforcement and the net flow of Mexican illegal migration. Discussion Paper No. 1642, Institute for the Study of Labor (IZA), Bonn, Germany.

Antecol, Heather, Deborah A. Cobb-Clark, and Stephen J. Trejo. 2003. Immigration policy and the skills of immigrants to Australia, Canada, and the United States. *Journal of Human Resources* 38 (1): 192–218.

Aydemir, Abdurrahman, and George J. Borjas. 2007. Cross-country variation in the impact of international migration: Canada, Mexico, and the United States. *Journal of the European Economic Association* 5 (4): 663–708.

Aydemir, Abdurrahman, and Mikal Skuterud. 2005. Explaining the deteriorating entry earnings of Canada's immigrant cohorts, 1966–2000. *Canadian Journal of Economics* 38 (2): 641–71.

Banerjee, Rupa. 2008. An examination of factors affecting perception of workplace discrimination. *Journal of Labor Research* 29 (4): 380–401.

Bansak, Cynthia, and Stephen Raphael. 2001. Immigration reform and the earnings of Latino workers: Do employer sanctions cause discrimination? *Industrial and Labor Relations Review* 54 (2): 275–95.

Barrett, Alan. 1996. The greencard lottery winners: Are they more or less skilled than other immigrants? *Economics Letters* 52 (3): 331–35.

Batson, Andrew, and Andrew Browne. 2009. Wen voices concern over China's U.S. Treasurys. *Wall Street Journal*, March 13. http://online.wsj.com/article/SB123692233477317069.html.

Bean, Frank D., Jennifer Van Hook, James Bachmeier, and Mark A. Leach. 2007. Internal migration in the young adult foreign-born population of the United States, 1995–2000. Immigration Studies Whitepaper, Sabre Systems. http://www.sabresystems.com/whitepapers/EMS2_Deliverable%204.4_NIM_071207.pdf.

Becker, Gary S. 1987. Why not let immigrants pay for speedy entry? *Business Week*, March 2.

Benhabib, Jess, and Boyan Jovanovic. 2007. Optimal migration: A world perspective. Working Paper No. 12871, National Bureau of Economic Research, Cambridge, MA.

Bhagwati, Jagdish N., ed. 1976. *The brain drain and taxation: Theory and empirical analysis*, Vol. 2. Amsterdam: North-Holland.

Bodvarsson, Örn B., and Hendrik Van den Berg. 2009. *The economics of immigration: Theory and policy.* London: Springer.

Bodvarsson, Örn B., Hendrik F. Van den Berg, and Joshua J. Lewer. 2008. Measuring immigration's effects on labor demand: A reexamination of the Mariel boatlift. *Labour Economics* 15 (August 2008): 560–74.

Borjas, George J. 1987. Self-selection and the earnings of immigrants. *American Economic Review* 77 (4): 531–53.

———. 1999a. The economic analysis of immigration. In *Handbook of labor economics,* Vol. 3A, ed. Orley Ashenfelter and David Card, 1697–1760. Amsterdam: Elsevier.

———. 1999b. Heaven's door: Immigration policy and the American economy. Princeton, NJ: Princeton University Press.

———. 2003. The labor demand curve is downward sloping: Reexamining the impact of immigration on the labor market. *Quarterly Journal of Economics* 118 (4): 1335–74.

———, and Bernt Bratsberg. 1996. Who leaves? The outmigration of the foreign-born. *Review of Economics and Statistics* 78 (1): 165–76.

Borjas, George J., Richard B. Freeman, and Lawrence F. Katz. 1997. How much do immigration and trade affect labor market outcomes? *Brookings Papers on Economic Activity* 1: 1–67.

Borjas, George J., Jeffrey Grogger, and Gordon H. Hanson. 2008. Imperfect substitution between immigrants and natives: A reappraisal. Working Paper No. 13887, National Bureau of Economic Research, Cambridge, MA.

Borjas, George J., and Lawrence F. Katz. 2007. The evolution of the Mexican-born workforce in the United States. In *Mexican immigration to the United States,* ed. George J. Borjas, 13–56. Chicago: University of Chicago Press.

Bound, John, Sarah Turner, and Patrick Walsh. 2009. Internationalization of U.S. doctorate education. Working Paper No. 14792, National Bureau of Economic Research, Cambridge, MA.

Brown, J. David, Julie L. Hotchkiss, and Myriam Quispe-Agnoli. 2009. Undocumented worker employment and firm survival. Discussion Paper No. 3936, Institute for the Study of Labor (IZA), Bonn, Germany.

Brücker, Herbert, Gil S. Epstein, Barry McCormick, Gilles Saint-Paul, Alessandra Venturini, and Klaus Zimmermann. 2002. Part 1: Managing Migration in the European Welfare State. In *Immigration Policy and the Welfare System,* ed. Tito Boeri, Gordon Hanson, and Barry McCormick, 1–151. Oxford: Oxford University Press.

Capps, Randy, and Karina Fortuny. 2006. Immigration and child and family policy. Urban Institute, Washington, DC. http://www.urban.org/publications/311362.html.

Card, David. 2001. Immigrant inflows, native outflows, and the local labor market impacts of higher immigration. *Journal of Labor Economics* 19 (1): 22–64.

———. 2009. Immigration and inequality. *American Economic Review: Papers & Proceedings* 99 (2): 1–22.

Carrion–Flores, Carmen, and Todd Sorensen. 2009. The effects of border enforcement on migrants' border crossing choices: Diversion, or deterrence? Mimeo. Department of Economics, University of California, Riverside.

Chellaraj, Gnanaraj, Keith E. Maskus, and Aaditya Mattoo. 2005. The contribution of skilled immigration and international graduate students to U.S. innovation. Working Paper No. 3588, World Bank, Washington, DC.

Chiquiar, Daniel, and Gordon H. Hanson. 2005. International migration, self-selection, and the distribution of wages: Evidence from Mexico and the United States. *Journal of Political Economy* 113 (2): 239–81.

Chiswick, Barry R. 1982. The impact of immigration on the level and distribution of economic well–being. In *The gateway: U.S. immigration issues and policies,* ed. Barry R. Chiswick, 289–313. Washington, DC: American Enterprise Institute.

———.1999. Are immigrants favorably self–selected? *American Economic Review: Papers & Proceedings* 89 (2): 181–85.

———, Anh T. Le, and Paul W. Miller. 2008. How immigrants fare across the earnings distribution in Australia and the United States. *Industrial and Labor Relations Review* 61 (3): 353–73.

Chiswick, Barry R., and Paul W. Miller. 2008. Occupational attainment and immigrant economic progress in Australia. *Economic Record* 84: S45–S56.

Citizenship and Immigration Canada. 2008. *Facts and figures: Immigration overview, permanent and temporary residents, 2007.* Ottawa: Citizenship and Immigration Canada. http://www.cic.gc.ca/ENGLISH/pdf/pub/facts2007.pdf.

Clemens, Michael, Claudio E. Montenegro, and Lant Pritchett. 2008. The place premium: Wage differences for identical workers across the U.S. border. Working Paper No. 148, Center for Global Development, Washington, DC.

Commander, Simon, Mark Kangasniemi, and L. Alan Winters. 2004. The brain drain: Curse or boon? A survey of the literature. In *Challenges to globalization: Analyzing the economics*, ed. Robert E. Baldwin and L. Alan Winters, 235–78. Chicago: University of Chicago Press.

Commission on Professionals in Science and Technology. 2005. *The foreign born in science and technology.* Washington, DC: Commission on Professionals in Science and Technology. https://www.cpst.org/STEM/STEM4_Report.pdf.

Congressional Budget Office. 2006. *Congressional Budget Office cost estimate, S.2611, Comprehensive Immigration Reform Act of 2006.* Washington, DC: Congressional Budget Office. http://www.cbo.gov/ftpdocs/72xx/doc7208/s2611.pdf (accessed May 22, 2009).

———. 2007a. *Congressional Budget Office cost estimate, Senate Amendment 1150 to S. 1348, The Comprehensive Immigration Reform Act of 2007.* Washington, DC: Congressional Budget Office. http://www.cbo.gov/ftpdocs/81xx/doc8179/SA1150_June4.pdf (accessed May 22, 2009).

———. 2007b. *The impact of undocumented immigrants on the budgets of state and local governments.* Washington, DC: Government Printing Office. http://www.cbo.gov/ftpdocs/87xx/doc8711/12–6–Immigration.pdf (accessed May 5, 2009).

Congressional Research Service. 2002. *Immigration: Adjustment to permanent resident status under Section 245(i)*, by Andorra Bruno. Washington, DC: Government Printing Office.

———. 2007. *Immigration: Legislative issues on nonimmigrant professional specialty (H–1B) workers*, by Ruth E. Wasem. Washington, DC: Government Printing Office.

Cortes, Patricia. 2008. The effect of low-skilled immigration on U.S. prices: Evidence from CPI data. *Journal of Political Economy* 116 (3): 381–422.

———, and José Tessada. 2008. Cheap maids and nannies: How low-skilled immigration is changing the labor supply of high-skilled American women. Mimeo. University of Chicago Graduate School of Business.

Council of Economic Advisers. 2007. *Immigration's economic impact*. Washington, DC: Government Printing Office.

Daniels, Roger. 2004. *Guarding the golden door: American immigration policy and immigrants since 1882*. New York: Hill and Wang.

DiNardo, John, Nicole M. Fortin, and Thomas Lemieux. 1996. Labor market institutions and the distribution of wages, 1973–1992: A semiparametric approach. *Econometrica* 64 (5): 1001–44.

Docquier, Frédéric, and Hillel Rapoport. 2009. Skilled immigration: The perspective of developing countries. In *Skilled immigration today*, ed. Jagdish Bhagwati and Gordon Hanson, 247–84. New York: Oxford University Press.

Eschbach, Karl, Jacqueline Hagan, Nestor Rodriquez, Ruben Hernandez-Leon, and Stanley Bailey. 1999. Death at the border. *International Migration Review* 33 (2): 430–54.

Fajnzylber, Pablo, and J. Humberto López, eds. 2008. *Remittances and development: Lessons from Latin America*. Washington, DC: World Bank.

Federal Reserve Bank of Dallas. 2006. *The best of all worlds: Globalizing the knowledge economy*. Annual report. Federal Reserve Bank of Dallas.

Fortuny, Karina, Randy Capps, and Jeffrey S. Passel. 2007. *The characteristics of unauthorized immigrants in California, Los Angeles County, and the United States*. Washington, DC: Urban Institute.

Freeman, Richard B. 2006. People flows in globalization. *Journal of Economic Perspectives* 20 (2): 145–70.

Friedberg, Rachel M., and Jennifer Hunt. 1995. The impact of immigrants on host country wages, employment and growth. *Journal of Economic Perspectives* 9 (2): 23–44.

Friedman, Milton. 1998. Milton Friedman: Soothsayer. Interview by Peter Brimelow. *Hoover Digest* 2 (1998).

———. 2006. Rose and Milton Friedman: The romance of economics. Interview by Tunku Varadarajan. *Wall Street Journal*, July 22.

Furtado, Delia, and Heinrich Hock. 2008. Immigration labor, child-care services, and the work-fertility trade-off in the United States. Discussion Paper No. 3506, Institute for the Study of Labor (IZA), Bonn, Germany.

Glaeser, Edward L., and Albert Saiz. 2003. The rise of the skilled city. Working Paper No. 10191, National Bureau of Economic Research, Cambridge, MA.

Goldin, Claudia, and Lawrence F. Katz. 2007. Long-run changes in the wage structure: Narrowing, widening, polarizing. *Brookings Papers on Economic Activity* 2: 135–65.

Goyle, Rajeev, and David A. Jaeger. 2005. *Deporting the undocumented: A cost assessment.* Washington, DC: Center for American Progress. http://www.americanprogress.org/kf/deporting_the_undocumented.pdf.

Hanson, Gordon H. 2005. *Why does immigration divide America? Public finance and political opposition to open borders.* Washington, DC: Institute for International Economics.

———. 2007. Emigration, labor supply, and earnings in Mexico. In *Mexican immigration to the United States,* ed. George Borjas, 289–328. Chicago: University of Chicago Press.

———. 2008. The economic consequences of the international migration of labor. Working Paper No. 14490, National Bureau of Economic Research, Cambridge, MA.

———. 2009. The governance of migration policy. Human Development Reports Research Paper 2009/2, United Nations Development Program, New York.

———, Kenneth F. Scheve, Matthew J. Slaughter, and Antonio Spilimbergo. 2002. Immigration and the US economy: Labor-market impacts, illegal entry, and policy choices. In *Immigration policy and the welfare system,* ed. Tito Boeri, Gordon Hanson, and Barry McCormick, 169–285. Oxford: Oxford University Press.

Hanson, Gordon H., and Antonio Spilimbergo. 1999. Illegal immigration, border enforcement, and relative wages: Evidence from apprehensions at the U.S.-Mexico border. *American Economic Review* 89 (5): 1337–57.

Hatton, Timothy J. 2007. Should we have a WTO for international migration? *Economic Policy* 50: 339–83.

———, and Jeffrey G. Williamson. 1998. *The age of mass migration: Causes and economic impact.* New York: Oxford University Press.

———. 2005. A dual policy paradox: Why have trade and immigration policies always differed in labor-scarce countries? Working Paper No. 11866, National Bureau of Economic Research, Cambridge, MA.

———. 2009. Vanishing third world emigrants? Working Paper No. 14785, National Bureau of Economic Research, Cambridge, MA.

Heisler, Barbara Schmitter. 2002. New and old immigrant minorities in Germany: The challenge of incorporation. In *West European immigration and immigrant policy in the new century,* ed. Anthony M. Messina, 123–40. Westport, CT: Praeger.

Hill, Laura, Magnus Lofstrom, and Joseph Hayes. 2010. Immigrant legalization: Assessing the labor market effects. Public Policy Institute of California, San Francisco, CA.

Hoefer, Michael D. 1991. Background of U.S. immigration policy reform. In *U.S. immigration policy reform in the 1980s,* ed. Francisco L. Rivera-Batiz, Selig L. Sechzer, and Ira N. Gang, 17–44. New York: Praeger.

Holmes, Thomas J., and James A. Schmitz, Jr. 1994. Resistance to technology and trade between areas. Staff Report 184, Federal Reserve Bank of Minneapolis.

————. 1998. A gain from trade: More research, less obstruction. Staff Report 245, Federal Reserve Bank of Minneapolis.

Hoover Institution. 1997. *Immigration and the rise and decline of American cities.* Palo Alto, CA: Hoover Institution.

Hummels, David. 2007. Transportation costs and international trade in the second era of globalization. *Journal of Economic Perspectives* 21 (3): 131–54.

Hunt, Jennifer. 2009. Which immigrants are most innovative and entrepreneurial? Distinctions by entry visa. Working Paper No. 14920, National Bureau of Economic Research, Cambridge, MA.

————, and Marjolaine Gauthier-Lauselle. 2008. How much does immigration boost innovation? Working Paper No. 14312, National Bureau of Economic Research, Cambridge, MA.

Isbister, John. 1996. *The immigration debate: Remaking America.* West Hartford, CT: Kumarian Press.

Jasso, Guillermina. 2009. What do we expect from our government representatives on immigration? Mimeo, Department of Sociology, New York University, New York.

————, Douglas S. Massey, Mark R. Rosenzweig, and James P. Smith. 2000. The New Immigrant Survey Pilot (NIS–P): Overview and new findings about U.S. legal immigrants at admission. *Demography* 39 (1): 127–38.

Jasso, Guillermina, and Mark R. Rosenzweig. 1982. Estimating the emigration rates of legal immigrants using administrative and survey data: The 1971 cohort of immigrants to the United States. *Demography* 19 (3): 279–90.

————. 2009. Selection criteria and the skill composition of immigrants: A comparative analysis of Australian and U.S. employment immigration. In *Skilled immigration today: Prospects, problems, and policies,* ed. Jagdish Bhagwati and Gordon Hanson, 153–83. New York: Oxford University Press.

Kandilov, Amy M. Gass, and Ivan T. Kandilov. 2009. The effect of legalization on wages and health insurance: Evidence from the National Agricultural Workers Survey. Paper presented at Society of Labor Economists annual meeting, Boston, May.

Karoly, Lynn A., and Constantijn W. A. Panis. 2009. Supply of and demand for skilled labor in the United States. In *Skilled immigration today: Prospects, problems, and policies,* ed. Jagdish Bhagwati and Gordon Hanson, 15–52. New York: Oxford University Press.

Kerr, William R. 2008. Ethnic scientific communities and international technology diffusion. *Review of Economics and Statistics* 90 (3): 518–37.

————, and William F. Lincoln. 2008. The supply side of innovation: H-1B visa reforms and US ethnic invention. Working Paper 09–005, Harvard Business School, Cambridge, MA.

Klemperer, Paul. 2002. What really matters in auction design. *Journal of Economic Perspectives* 16 (1): 169–89.

Kossoudji, Sherrie, and Deborah A. Cobb-Clark. 2002. Coming out of the shadows: Learning about legal status and wages from the legalized population. *Journal of Labor Economics* 20 (3): 598–628.

Ku, Leighton. 2006. *Why immigrants lack adequate access to health care and health insurance.* Washington, DC: Migration Information Source. http://www.migrationinformation.org/Feature/display.cfm?id=417.

Lane, Philip R., and Gian Maria Milesi-Ferretti. 2006. The external wealth of nations mark II: Revised and extended estimates of foreign assets and liabilities, 1970–2004. Working Paper 06/69, International Monetary Fund, Washington, DC.

Lewis, Ethan G. 2005. Immigration, skill mix, and the choice of technique. Working Paper No. 05–08, Federal Reserve Bank of Philadelphia.

Longhi, Simonetta, Peter Nijkamp, and Jacques Poot. 2005. A meta-analytic assessment of the effect of immigration on wages. *Journal of Economic Surveys* 19 (3): 451–77.

Lowell, B. Lindsay, Jay Teachman, and Shongren Jing. 1995. Unintended consequences of immigration reform: Discrimination and Hispanic employment. *Demography* 32 (4): 617–28.

Lucas, Robert. 1990. Why doesn't capital flow from rich to poor countries? *American Economic Review* 80 (2): 92–96.

Martin, Phil. 2007. *Farm labor shortages: How real? What response?* Washington, DC: Center for Immigration Studies. http://www.cis.org/articles/2007/back907.pdf.

Martin, Susan, B. Lindsay Lowell, and Micah Bump. 2009. Skilled immigration to America: U.S. admission policies in the 21st century. In *Skilled immigration today: Prospects, problems, and policies*, ed. Jagdish Bhagwati and Gordon Hanson, 131–52. New York: Oxford University Press.

Massey, Douglas S., Joaquin Arango, Graeme Hugo, Ali Kouaouci, Adela Pellegrino, and J. Edward Taylor. 1999. *Worlds in motion: Understanding international migration at the end of the millennium.* Oxford: Oxford University Press.

Massey, Douglas S., Jorge Durand, and Nolan J. Malone. 2002. *Beyond smoke and mirrors: Mexican immigration in an era of economic integration.* New York: Russell Sage Foundation.

Massey, Douglas S., and Audrey Singer. 1995. New estimates of undocumented Mexican migration and the probability of apprehension. *Demography* 32 (2): 203–13.

Mayr, Karin, and Giovanni Peri. 2008. Return migration as a channel of brain gain. Working Paper No. 14039, National Bureau of Economic Research, Cambridge, MA.

Migration Dialogue. 2002. Muslims, 245i, airports. *Migration News* 8, no. 4 (May). http://migration.ucdavis.edu/mn/more.php?id=2615_0_2_0.

Migration Policy Institute. 2006. *Immigration and America's future: A new chapter.* Washington, DC: Migration Policy Institute.

Milgrom, Paul. 1989. Auctions and bidding: A primer. *Journal of Economic Perspectives* 3 (3): 3–22.

Miller, Paul W., and Leanne M. Neo. 2003. Labour market flexibility and immigrant adjustment. *Economic Record* 79 (246): 336–56.

Millman, Joel. 1997. *The other Americans: How immigrants renew our country, our economy, and our values.* New York: Penguin.

Mishra, Prachi. 2007. Emigration and wages in source countries: Evidence from Mexico. *Journal of Development Economics* 82 (1): 180–99.

Mohanty, Sarita A., Steffie Woolhandler, David U. Himmelstein, Susmita Pati, Olveen Carrasquillo, and David H. Bor. 2005. Health care expenditures of immigrants in the United States: A nationally representative analysis. *American Journal of Public Health* 95 (8): 1–8.

Mokyr, Joel. 1990. *The lever of riches: Technological creativity and economic progress.* New York: Oxford University Press.

Mora-Torres, Juan. 2001. *The making of the Mexican border: The state, capitalism and the border in Nuevo Leon, 1848–1910.* Austin: University of Texas Press.

National Research Council. Committee on Science, Security and Prosperity. 2009. *Beyond fortress America.* Washington, DC: National Academies Press.

OECD. 2008. *International migration outlook: 2008 edition.* Paris: OECD Publishing.

———. 2009a. *Education at a glance 2009: OECD indicators.* Paris: OECD Publishing.

———. 2009b. Total fertility rates. http://www.oecd.org/dataoecd/44/34/37962718.pdf.

Office of Management and Budget. 2007. Budget of the United States Government, 2008. http://www.whitehouse.gov/omb/budget/fy2008/homeland.html.

———. 2008. Budget of the United States Government. 2009. http://www.whitehouse.gov/omb/budget/fy2009/homeland.html.

Orrenius, Pia M. 1999. Return migration from Mexico: Theory and evidence. Ph.D. diss., University of California, Los Angeles.

———, and Genevieve R. Solomon. 2006. How labor market policies shape immigrants' opportunities. *Economic Letter* (Federal Reserve Bank of Dallas) 1 (7): 1–8.

Orrenius, Pia M., and Daniel Streitfeld. 2006. TN visas: A stepping stone toward a NAFTA labor market. *Southwest Economy* (Federal Reserve Bank of Dallas) 6 (November/December): 10–13.

Orrenius, Pia M., and Madeline Zavodny. 2005. Self-selection and undocumented immigrants from Mexico. *Journal of Development Economics* 78 (1): 215–40.

———. 2007. Does immigration affect wages? A look at occupation-level evidence. *Labour Economics* 14 (5): 757–73.

———. 2009. The effect of tougher enforcement on the job prospects of recent Latin American immigrants. *Journal of Policy Analysis and Management* 28 (2): 239–57.

Ottaviano, Gianmarco I. P., and Giovanni Peri. 2008. Immigration and national wages: clarifying the theory and the empirics. Working Paper No. 14188, National Bureau of Economic Research, Cambridge, MA

Papademetriou, Demetrios G. 2005. *The global struggle with illegal migration: No end in sight.* Washington, DC: Migration Policy Institute.

———, Doris Meissner, Mark R. Rosenblum, and Madeleine Sumption. 2009. *Harnessing the advantages of immigration for a 21st-century economy: A standing commission on labor markets, economic competitiveness, and immigration.* Washington, DC: Migration Policy Institute.

Papademetriou, Demetrios, Will Somerville, and Hiroyuki Tanaka. 2008. Hybrid immigrant-selection systems: The next generation of economic migration schemes. Working Paper, November 2008, Transatlantic Council on Migration, Migration Policy Institute, Washington, DC.

Park, Edward J. W. 2007. "Unworthy of a nation built by immigrants": The political mobilization of H-1B workers. In *Movement of global talent: The impact of high skill labor flows from India and China,* ed. Udai Tambar, 75–88. Princeton, NJ: Research Policy Institute for the Region, Woodrow Wilson School of Public and International Affairs, Princeton University.

Passel, Jeffrey S. 2005. *Unauthorized migrants: Numbers and characteristics.* Washington, DC: Pew Hispanic Center. http://pewhispanic.org/files/reports/46.pdf.

———, and D'Vera Cohn. 2008a. *Trends in unauthorized immigration: Undocumented inflow now trails legal inflow.* Washington, DC: Pew Hispanic Center. http://pewhispanic.org/files/reports/94.pdf.

———. 2008b. *U.S. population projections, 2005–2050.* Washington, DC: Pew Hispanic Center. http://pewhispanic.org/files/reports/85.pdf.

———. 2009. *A portrait of unauthorized immigrants in the United States.* Washington, DC: Pew Hispanic Center. http://pewhispanic.org/files/reports/107.pdf.

Passel, Jeffrey S., and Roberto Suro. 2005. *Rise, peak and decline: Trends in U.S. immigration 1992–2004.* Washington, DC: Pew Hispanic Center. http://pewhispanic.org/files/reports/53.pdf.

Picot, Garnett, Feng Hou, and Simon Coulombe. 2007. Chronic low income and low–income dynamics among recent immigrants. Research Paper No. 294, Statistics Canada, Ottawa, Ontario.

Piore, Michael J. 1979. *Birds of passage: Migrant labor and industrial society.* Cambridge: Cambridge University Press.

Porter, Michael E. 1998. The Adam Smith Address: Location, clusters, and the "new" microeconomics of competition. *Business Economics* 33 (1): 7–14.

Portes, Alejandro, ed. 1995. *The economic sociology of immigration: Essays on networks, ethnicity, and entrepreneurship.* New York: Russell Sage Foundation.

Pritchett, Lant. 2006. *Let their people come: Breaking the gridlock on international labor mobility.* Washington, DC: Center for Global Development.

Public Policy Institute of California. 2008. *Just the facts: Immigrant admissions: Family versus skills.* San Francisco: Public Policy Institute of California. http://www.ppic.org/content/pubs/jtf/JTF_ImmigrantAdmissionsJTF.pdf.

Rapoport, Hillel, and Frédéric Docquier. 2006. The economics of migrants' remittances. In *Handbook of the economics of giving, altruism and reciprocity,* Vol. 2, ed. Serge-Christophe Kolm and Jean Ythier, 1135–1200. Amsterdam: Elsevier.

Ratha, Dilip. 2007. Leveraging remittances for development. Policy Brief, Migration Policy Institute, Washington, DC. http://www.migrationpolicy.org/pubs/MigDevPB_062507.pdf.

————, and Sanket Mohapatra. 2009. Revised outlook for remittance flows 2009–2011. Migration and Development Brief No. 9, World Bank, Washington, DC. http://siteresources.worldbank.org/INTPROSPECTS/Resources/MD_Brief9_Mar2009.pdf.

Reyes, Belinda I. 2004. U.S. immigration policy and the duration of undocumented trips. In *Crossing the border: Research from the Mexican Migration Project,* ed. Jorge Durand and Douglas Massey, 299–320. New York: Russell Sage Foundation.

Riosmena, Fernando. 2004. Return versus settlement among undocumented Mexican migrations, 1980 to 1996. In *Crossing the border: Research from the Mexican Migration Project,* ed. Jorge Durand and Douglas Massey, 265–80. New York: Russell Sage Foundation.

Rivera-Batiz, Francisco L. 1999. Undocumented workers in the labor market: An analysis of the earnings of legal and illegal Mexican immigrants in the United States. *Journal of Population Economics* 12 (1): 91–116.

Rodrik, Dani. 2001. Comments at the conference "Immigration Policy and the Welfare State," Trieste, Italy. http://ksghome.harvard.edu/~drodrik/papers.html.

————. 2005. Feasible globalizations. In *Globalization: What's new,* ed. Michael M. Weinstein, 196–213. New York: Columbia University Press.

Rosenzweig, Mark. 2007. Education and migration: A global perspective. Mimeo. Department of Economics, Yale University, New Haven, CT.

Sachs, Jeffrey D. 2008. *Common wealth: Economics for a crowded planet.* New York: Penguin Books.

Saiz, Albert. 2007. Immigration and housing rents in American cities. *Journal of Urban Economics* 61 (2): 345–71.

Saxenian, AnnaLee. 2006. *The new argonauts.* Cambridge, MA: Harvard University Press.

————, and K. M. Shin. 2006. Immigration and the transformation of the Silicon Valley economy: 1970–2000. Unpublished paper, University of California, Berkeley.

Scheve, Kenneth F., and Matthew J. Slaughter. 2001. Labor-market competition and individual preferences over immigration policy. *Review of Economics and Statistics* 83 (1): 133–45.

————. 2007. A new deal for globalization. *Foreign Affairs* 86 (4): 34–47.

Schumpeter, Joseph A. 1934. *The theory of economic development.* Cambridge, MA: Harvard University Press.

Simon, Julian L. 1989. *The economic consequences of immigration.* Cambridge, MA: Basil Blackwell.

Small Business Administration. 2008. *Estimating the contribution of immigrant business owners to the U.S. economy,* by Robert W. Fairlie. Washington, DC: Government Printing Office.

Smith, James P., and Barry Edmonston, ed. 1997. *The new Americans: Economic, demographic, and fiscal effects of immigration.* Washington, DC: National Academies Press.

Tichenor, Daniel. 2002. *Dividing lines: The politics of immigration control in America.* Princeton, NJ: Princeton University Press.

Tiebout, Charles. 1956. A pure theory of local expenditures. *Journal of Political Economy* 64 (5): 416–26.

United Nations. Department of Economic and Social Affairs. Population Division. 2006. *Trends in total migrant stock: The 2005 revision.* New York: United Nations.

———. 2008. *International migrant stock: The 2008 revision.* New York: United Nations. http://esa.un.org/migration/index.asp?panel=1.

United Nations High Commissioner for Refugees. 2007. *2007 Global trends.* http://www.unhcr.org/cgi-bin/texis/vtx/search?page=search&docid=4852366f2&query=global%20trends%202007.

United Nations Population Fund. 2006. *State of world population 2006.* http://www.unfpa.org/swp/2006/english/chapter_1/index.html.

U.S. Bureau of the Census. 2003. *Migration of natives and foreign born: 1995 to 2000.* Census 2000 Special Reports No. 11. http://www.census.gov/prod/2003pubs/censr–11.pdf.

———. 2010. Foreign trade statistics. http://www.census.gov/indicator/www/ustrade.html (accessed March 9, 2010).

U.S. Bureau of the Census. Population Division. 1999. Historical statistics on the foreign-born population of the United States: 1850–1990. By Campbell J. Gibson and Emily Lennon. Population Division Working Paper No. 29. http://www.census.gov/population/www/documentation/twps0029/twps0029.html.

U.S. Bureau of Labor Statistics. 2009. *Occupational outlook handbook, 2008-09 Edition.* Washington, DC: Bureau of Labor Statistics. http://www.bls.gov/oco/oco2003.htm.

U.S. Citizenship and Immigration Service. 2008a. Memorandum from Donald Neufeld to field leadership. Revisions to adjudicator's field manual. http://www.uscis.gov/files/nativedocuments/AC21_30May08.pdf.

———. 2008b. USCIS runs random selection process for H-1B petitions. http://www.uscis.gov/portal/site/uscis/menuitem.5af9bb95919f35e66f61417654 3f6d1a/?vgnextoid=183f301458e49110VgnVCM1000004718190aRCRD&vg nextchannel=b56db6f2cae63110VgnVCM1000004718190aRCRD.

———. 2010. USCIS processing time information. https://egov.uscis.gov/cris/processTimesDisplay.do;jsessionid=bac585.

U.S. Department of Homeland Security. Office of Immigration Statistics. 2009a. *U.S. Legal Permanent Residents, 2008,* by Randall Monger and Nancy Rytina. http://www.dhs.gov/xlibrary/assets/statistics/publications/lpr_fr_2008.pdf (accessed May 5, 2009).

———. 2009b. *Yearbook of immigration statistics: 2008.* http://www.dhs.gov/ximgtn/statistics/publications/LPR08.shtm.

———. 2010. *Estimates of the unauthorized immigrant population residing in the United States: January 2009,* by Michael Hoefer, Nancy Rytina, and Bryan C. Baker. http://www.dhs.gov/xlibrary/assets/statistics/publications/ois_ill_pe_2009.pdf.

U.S. Department of Labor. 2004. Aging baby boomers in a new workforce development system. http://www.doleta.gov/Seniors/other_docs/AgingBoomers.pdf.

U.S. Department of State. 2009a. *Visa Bulletin* 8, no. 6 (March). http://travel.state.gov/visa/frvi/bulletin/bulletin_4428.html.

———. 2009b. *Visa Bulletin* 9, no. 7 (April). http://travel.state.gov/visa/frvi/bulletin/bulletin_4438.html.

U.S. Immigration and Customs Enforcement. 2009. *Worksite enforcement overview.* http://www.ice.gov/pi/news/factsheets/worksite.htm (accessed May 26, 2009).

U.S. Immigration and Naturalization Service. 1951. *Annual report, 1951.* http://ia311233.us.archive.org/2/items/annualreportofim1951unit/annualreportofim1951unit.pdf.

———. 2002. *Immigrants admitted into the United States as legal permanent residents, FY 2000.* Public use data file. NTIS order no. PB2002-500064.

Wadhwa, Vivek, Gary Gereffi, Ben Rissing, and AnnaLee Saxenian. 2007. America's new immigrant entrepreneurs. Science, Technology, and Innovation Paper No. 23, Duke University, Durham, NC.

Wadhwa, Vivek, Guillermina Jasso, Ben Rissing, Gary Gereffi, and Richard Freeman. 2007. *Intellectual property, the immigration backlog, and a reverse brain-drain: America's new immigrant entrepreneurs, part III.* Kansas City, MO: Kauffman Foundation.

Warren, Robert, and Jennifer Marks Peck. 1980. Foreign-born emigration from the United States: 1960 to 1970. *Demography* 17 (1): 71–84.

World Bank. 2006a. *Global economic prospects 2006: Economic implications of remittances and migration.* Washington, DC: World Bank.

———. 2006b. *Where is the wealth of nations? Measuring capital for the 21st century.* Washington, DC: World Bank.

———. 2008. Migration and remittances factbook. http://econ.worldbank.org/WBSITE/EXTERNAL/EXTDEC/EXTDECPROSPECTS/0,,contentMDK:21352016~pagePK:64165401~piPK:64165026~theSitePK:476883,00.html (accessed October 7, 2009).

———. 2009. *World development indicators.* Washington, DC: World Bank.

Wynne, Mark. 2009. Three lectures on globalization and financial services. Globalization and Monetary Policy Institute, Federal Reserve Bank of Dallas.

Zimmermann, Klaus F. 2009. Labor mobility and the integration of European labor markets. Discussion Paper No. 3999, Institute for the Study of Labor (IZA), Bonn, Germany.

Zweig, David. 2007. The mobility of Chinese human capital: The view from the United States. In *Movement of global talent: The impact of high skill labor flows from India and China,* ed. Udai Tambar, 9–22. Princeton, NJ: Research Policy Institute for the Region, Woodrow Wilson School of Public and International Affairs, Princeton University.

Index

About the Authors

Pia M. Orrenius is research officer and senior economist at the Federal Reserve Bank of Dallas and adjunct professor at the Hankamer School of Business, Baylor University. Dr. Orrenius is also a research fellow at the Tower Center for Political Studies at Southern Methodist University and at the Institute for the Study of Labor in Bonn. She was senior economist on the Council of Economic Advisers in 2004–2005. Her research focuses on the labor market impacts of immigration, illegal immigration, and U.S. immigration policy, and her work has appeared in the *Journal of Development Economics, Economic Theory, Labour Economics, Industrial and Labor Relations Review*, and *Demography*, among other publications. Dr. Orrenius received her PhD in economics from the University of California at Los Angeles and undergraduate degrees in economics and Spanish from the University of Illinois at Urbana-Champaign.

Madeline Zavodny is a professor of economics at Agnes Scott College in Decatur, Georgia, and a research fellow at the Institute for the Study of Labor in Bonn. She was formerly an associate professor of economics at Occidental College and a research economist at the Federal Reserve Bank of Atlanta and the Federal Reserve Bank of Dallas. Her research on the economics of immigration has been published in the *Journal of Labor Economics, Journal of Development Economics, Demography, Industrial and Labor Relations Review, Research in Labor Economics*, and *Journal of Policy Analysis and Management*. She received an undergraduate degree in economics from Claremont McKenna College and a PhD in economics from the Massachusetts Institute of Technology.